DEDICATION

To my brother, Ben Lewis, who lived at a time when medicine wasn't as advanced as it is today. At age forty-eight in 1994, he died of complications of AIDS.

As president of a bank and as a married man with a daughter, he led a double life until he became ill.

He really did not have a chance to live a fully open life and to be authentically true to himself.

In his memory it is my pleasure to share these inspirational stories of people in his community who were able to finally and joyfully live openly and as they wish.

INTRODUCTION

How individuals find the strength to live authentically and courageously when life presents difficult obstacles is a central theme of my work. In this book, the ribbons of steel in the photos represent life and reality. Just as these courageous LGBTQ people bend and shape steel in these photos, they tell in their own words of bending the realities of their lives to become the individuals they were meant to be.

Their stories relate no easy struggle to live in accordance with their gender identity and sexual orientation—essential elements of personal liberty, dignity, and autonomy. Where there was hate and rejection, they chose love. Where there was fear, they chose courage. When they faced falsehoods, they chose truth. When threatened, they chose a quiet resistance. And when isolated, they built community.

You'll recognize different personalities in the photos and stories: from outgoing and fun to introspective and serious, from insistent and in-your-face to sensitive and soft-spoken. But as their words and pictures demonstrate, they all are exuberantly alive.

I hope my photographs and the accompanying profiles will remind readers that we all experience joy, sadness, and hardships in our lives. We all want to live true to ourselves. And we all want to live without prejudice and hate.

Jan Dee Gordon

Alec Mapa

I found when I came out professionally, the way I'm bending steel, the way I'm bending reality, is by being who I am: a gay Filipino man working in television, the most mainstream thing ever.

I'm Filipino-American, born and raised in San Francisco.

I grew up in a very Catholic, conservative home during the permissive seventies. I was always gay. I was very effeminate. My father suffered from PTSD because of his service in World War II. He was prone to sudden uncontrollable rages. My survival mechanism was to make him laugh. I grew up with traumatized people, making them laugh. That became my personality, and it's how I learned to be loved.

My parents did not raise me to love being a gay person. That's a garden I have to weed every day, or the weeds grow back. I think that as a queer person, you have to learn how to parent yourself, and you have to make the choice to be you and *only you*.

There's no strength in conformity. Conformity is weakness. Conformity dilutes you. Conformity is making yourself smaller in order to make other people feel comfortable. Being your genuine self takes bravery.

I got bullied in school but not for being Asian—there were a lot of kids who looked like me—but for being gay. When I finally came out in high school and I was like, "I'm gay." There was nothing left to bully. It was like, "Hey, faggot." And I was like, "Yeah." And that would end it.

I found when I came out professionally, the way I'm bending steel, the way I'm bending reality, is by being who I am: a gay Filipino man working in television, the most mainstream thing ever. When I first came to town and tried to be what everybody else wanted me to be, I had nothing to bring to the table. There was nothing authentic. I was afraid to be myself. I was like, "I'm too gay, I'm too this, I'm too wrong." And so I would try to fit into the box, trying to conform. But then you just end up being in drag in a negative way and not a celebratory way. You're in a costume but your most colorful costume is yourself, your own skin.

So when I stopped worrying about what people thought of the *real me*, the exact opposite of what I thought would happen, happened: I worked all the time. I did series television. I was on *Ugly Betty*. I was on *Desperate Housewives*. I was on *Switched at Birth* and ABC Family. It's always delightful to be proven right.

I don't really use other people's opinions of me as a barometer of how I should feel about myself. And that's the most grown-up I'll ever be. However, there are still situations I find myself in where I need to understand who's going to be cool, who's going to be okay with me. On my very first network call for a sitcom, I was axed, and I knew who axed me. I saw an executive in the room with daggers coming out of his eyes. I could see them. I could feel them. My agent called me and said, "You're out of the running; *so-and-so* didn't like you." And I thought, "I knew it. I absolutely knew it; I'm done."

But my agent called again the next week and said that they haven't found anyone else and they wanted to see me again. So I had to go back into that room in front of that same executive who hated my guts. And he knew that I knew. So the first thing I said when I walked in was, "Hello, I guess a group hug is out of the question."

He laughed as if to say to me: "Fair enough, I didn't like you, but you got me." So I think that when you make people laugh, they can identify with you. That's the common ground.

I hosted a reality show for AMC called *Showville*, which took me to the most rural parts of America. So it's big Queenie me coming into these small towns. I found that everybody in America works really hard to be broke. There are smart people everywhere. The minute I made them laugh, I would see their defenses drop. I would see them melt, and it changed me too: it made me less fearful of those situations. If we could all get past our fear of each other and communicate, I think we'll find that we have more in common than we think we do.

I'm now included in places because I see myself as included. Your biggest obstacle is yourself. At the end of the day it's all in your head. It's *The Wizard of Oz*. You have the courage, the heart, the brains, but you have to kill the witch in order to figure that out.

And when you do that, nobody can take that away from you. ■

In the end it's all in your head.

How strong or weak
you're going to be
is up to you.

My name is Riley Buss-Drexel. I'm a full-time student and also work for Alaska Airlines as a flight attendant.

I'm now involved in leading a special project with the Los Angeles Lakers designed to reach out to the LGBTQ community. I've been asked to handle the planning and creative strategy for the first-ever Pride Night at a home game this coming season. Our goal is to help promote the team as a team for everyone, not just a select few, so that every person in LA feels some connection to the game of basketball.

My family, the Buss family, has been involved with the team for many years. My grandfather, Jerry Buss, was a long-time owner of the Lakers. When he died in 2013, the ownership was transferred to his children including my mom, Janie Buss, and my aunt, Jeanie Buss. Aunt Jeanie is the controlling owner and president. She represents the Lakers on the NBA Board of Governors.

I've never let the label *gay* affect me. But I have had to

So many people are driven by ulterior motives that can divide us. We need to create positive outcomes from our actions. We need to spread good in the world.

overcome the fear of not having acceptance from my family. And part of that was wanting to be a part of the Los Angeles Lakers organization, which has been such an important part of my upbringing and the Los Angeles community. There have been obstacles along the way, but I've been relentless in pushing to find my niche in the organization in a way that would make a difference.

I saw powerful role models in my aunt and my mom, who battled preconceived notions that women could not succeed in a male-dominated sports world. They overcame all the stereotypes and succeeded at the highest levels. And I'm blessed that my grandfather gave them the opportunity to be powerful women in sports.

I went on an African safari recently and observed how animals in the wild adapted to their surroundings. Everything I saw in nature was simple and uncomplicated. It made me think about my own life. I've always been afraid of trying to create simplicity in my life. When I returned from that trip, I deconstructed everything that was going on and began to focus on just a few priorities.

I wanted the Lakers outreach to be a top priority for me. I did some research and found six other NBA teams that have sponsored Pride Nights. I did a complete project proposal. And then I approached my Aunt Jeanie and said, "We

We inhale intentions and exhale expectations.

really need to do this. Here is all the research I've done."

And so that's how I became the creative director and over-all planner of Pride Night. Once I was able to focus on my priorities and not be slowed by a fear of rejection, I was able to meet that goal. A gay member of the family was now involved in an important community outreach for this world-class NBA franchise.

So many people are driven by ulterior motives that can divide us. We need to create positive outcomes from our actions. We need to spread good in the world. I inhale only good intentions and exhale only the good. If you allow bad intentions in, you will also exhale them.

Know that what's right for you is what's right for you. And as long as it's ethical and consensual, nobody should judge you.

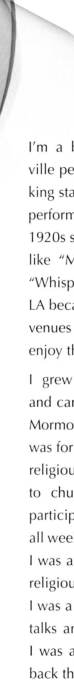

I'm a burlesque and vaudeville performer. With my drag king stage partner, I write and perform original songs in a 1920s style and cover classics like "My Blue Heaven" and "Whispering." I love living in LA because there are so many venues where people go to enjoy this kind of art.

I grew up in Provo, Utah, and came from a long line of Mormons. I grew up in what was for me a small, repressive religious enclave. I would go to church on Sundays and participate in church activities all week. And I was so devout. I was always at the top of my religious studies class. When I was a teenager, I would give talks and try to convert kids. I was a very different person back then.

I was raised to be a woman who would be subservient to men. That's how the Mormon religion works. Women are sec-ond-class citizens. I watched my mother and my sister be so subservient to their husbands, bowing to their every whim. And in my early twenties I was in a relationship like that. He was emotionally abusive, and sometimes physically abusive. And I would take it because I thought that's what women were supposed to do.

And so overcoming that mindset and becoming who I was meant to be was a huge challenge.

When I came to LA, I began to come into my own. I was blown away by the diversity of the people, the culture, and the subcultures that I found here. When I decided to perform burlesque, I adopted my stage name, Prix de Beauté, which I borrowed from the 1930 French film of the same name. It's about a woman performer. A talent agent wants to sign her to a movie contract. But her boyfriend is so controlling and jealous that he won't let her do it. So he keeps her locked up in her apartment. She keeps getting fan mail encouraging her to come out. And eventually she leaves him and begins to make her own life.

I related to her character because she overcame an abusive relationship and rebelled against the expectation that she would be a subservient woman.

I chose burlesque as the complete opposite of what was expected of me. I was told to be modest and pure, to wear garments that cover up almost everything. I was told that men own your body and eventually your husband will own your body. Burlesque empowered me. I did what I wanted to do with my body. I showed what I wanted to show; I had full control of how I would appear on stage. All that I was taught was bad I now embraced.

I identify as bisexual. I repressed those desires because of religion and my controlling boyfriend. But by my midtwenties I was able to explore my sexuality. I enjoyed both men and women romantically and sexually. I'm a proud bisexual. That word has been stigmatized lately. We are told we are cheaters, or we're going to go back to being straight, or we're really gay. I have a lot of bisexual friends who won't identify as bisexual; they'll go by queer or pan. But I think the word needs to be reclaimed, and I think we need to be proud they we're bisexual people.

All the pain and anger that came out of my earlier life ultimately pushed me to become the person I wanted to be. I don't believe in an afterlife. You need to do what you want to do and experience what you want to experience now. And that's where my strength comes from. By loving life and being who I want to be, I've become a successful performer. I produce my own shows. I've achieved a look I wanted to achieve. I've networked with people I've wanted to connect with.

I believe you can overcome most challenges by never questioning your intuition. Know that what's right for you is what's right for you. And as long as it's ethical and consensual, nobody should judge you. And don't be afraid of what people think. ∎

Sam Pancake

I'm Sam Pancake. I work as an actor, a comedian, and a writer. I do TV, movies, commercials, and a lot of stage work. My latest one-man show is called *Wasted on a Boy*, which is about my last thirty years as an out gay character actor working in Hollywood.

I grew up in a very large house with a big family in a very small town in West Virginia. There were six kids—three boys and three girls. The Pancakes had been in that county since the 1760s. My ancestors had lived in Germany and made pancakes. People, of course, think I made up my name to be a hilarious comedian.

The three of us older kids are gay—my two sisters and me. I knew when I was about four or five. My father was a minister and we would go after church to someone else's house for these giant, amazing southern luncheons. I remember going upstairs at the house we were visiting one Sunday, and the family's son was standing there in his underwear. He was about fifteen or sixteen, but to me this was a man. I was like, oh my God, like … that's for me. When I watched reruns of *The Beverly Hillbillies*, I liked Jethro not Elly May. I liked Burt Reynolds not Farrah Fawcett. So I always knew.

There was nothing worse in the sixties and seventies in rural West Virginia than being a gay kid. It was like *faggot* and *queer* and *homo*; it was a very masculine butch culture. I was terrified that somebody would find out I was gay and beat me up or kill me. I thought about suicide all the time. I escaped into fantasy. I remember seeing *Mary Poppins* and just escaping into that world. My mom was an art teacher, so there were art supplies in the house. I was drawing my way out of it constantly. I realize now I was just designing my own little world. I didn't know if I wanted to be an architect, an actor, or an artist. I just wanted people to like me and to make them laugh. So if they ever found out I was gay, they wouldn't want to kill me.

When I went to college in the early eighties to study theater, I started to find my people. I didn't come out of the closet until my senior year of college. I eventually told my sisters. And we talked about coming out to my parents, and they were like, "Just don't." My parents knew; we just never had the conversation. We didn't talk about a lot of stuff.

My greatest challenge, though, was overcoming a drug and alcohol addiction. I was a good example of a progressive alcoholic. I started drinking in high school, and I drank a lot through college. I worked very hard but I was always a party boy. As I started making more money as an actor, I started doing a lot of speed, crystal meth. It's terrifying. When I started I was like, "This keeps me up all night, and then I can just drink more." And because I loved to socialize, I was always throwing parties. I was just fun, fun, fun. Go, go, go.

By 2011 my drinking was starting to be problematic. By 2012 I entered rehab and came out. I've been sober ever since. Once I got all the chemicals out of my system during my first year of sobriety, I was able to say, "Oh, this is who I am."

I always believed in a higher power and had a strong spiritual practice. So plugging that into my recovery was easy, but it's ongoing. Here's the thing: I wanted to kill myself in the last days of my drinking. I was incredibly depressed and if there had been a gun in my bedroom, I probably wouldn't be here. I found out in sobriety that I don't have any naturally occurring depression. The pain I felt was due to all the alcohol. And today I'm also very lucky that I enjoy my company. I like to be around myself. I enjoy a wealth of relationships and friendships, but I am my own best friend.

I don't have any kids, but I am really pulling for that little boy back in West Virginia who was me then. I want to give him a good life. That's important for me because I just saw him so depressed and sad and broken and lonely and just emotionally exhausted and not getting the love he needed. So I make sure that I do well by him. I know that I can be of service to others in the best way possible by taking care of myself, by putting the oxygen mask on myself first before I put it on others. ■

*I feel the Meaning
of Life is the meaning
WE choose to give
our own lives, and
mine is to experience
and share as much
responsible
joy as possible.*

Calpernia Addams

I was born in 1971 in Nashville, Tennessee, which was in some ways a wonderful place to grow up—trees, creeks, farms. It was also very difficult in a lot of other ways. I grew up in a very strict fundamentalist Christian cult called the Church of God of Prophecy. We kept ourselves separated from the world. We weren't allowed to listen to modern music or watch movies. It left me without any cultural touchstones to talk about with my peers.

I'm trans. So I grew up being raised as a boy. My personality has always been the same. I was a shy, artistic, very feminine child. I grew up with the natural beauty of Tennessee and a deep love for my family juxtaposed with a deep-seated rejection of my softness and femininity and all my dreams and goals.

When I turned eighteen, I was told I would not go to college. And so I felt like my only escape from Tennessee was to join the military. I joined the Navy in 1990, which happened to be just as the first Gulf War was

I told myself that you really need to address your identity, be yourself, and be who you need to be.

unfolding, so I was quickly fast tracked. I had very high scores on my entrance tests, so I got to choose my job. I chose to be a medic, and I got more training as a field medical combat specialist, who is prepared to treat battlefield injuries and extreme trauma. It's a very intense job—crawling under the barbed wire, learning to fire bigger weapons, etc. And right after training, I was shipped off to Saudi Arabia to serve with the Marines who are supported by the Navy. And I was there for the whole war.

It may seem counterintuitive, but the military really took me in like family even as quirky as I was. I think they may have chalked it up to me just being so isolated; just this country rube, this hayseed who had never seen anything of the world. So the same type of rough boys who had bullied me and been mean to me in school took me under their wing in the military. And they sort of brought me into their fold. In the medical field it was okay that I was soft. And the rough guys knew that I might be saving their lives at some point. I made some wonderful friends and learned to be strong.

I lived for two years on an island in the Aleutian chain in Alaska. And for me that was a bit of the dark night of the soul. I realized then I could have died in the war. I told myself that you really need to address your identity, be yourself, and be who you need to be. I met a wonderful group of lesbians there who worked as mechanics on military airplanes. And they really helped me address my sexuality and my queer side.

So when my time in the military was up, I got out and I went back home and almost immediately found some trans women who mentored me. I began transition.

In 1999 I met a young man named Barry Winchell. I was out of the military by that time, but he was still in. We started a relationship as a boy and a girl, man and woman. And unfortunately his experience in the military was not mine. When they found out he was seeing a trans woman, he began to be bullied relentlessly and mercilessly. And on the Fourth of July, in 1999, they beat him to death in the barracks. And that's when my activism began.

Losing Barry was the worst thing that has ever happened to me because every other hardship was just a hill to climb that helped me become

Troubles are never over and life is never perfect, but you learn to deal with it and care less that it is not perfect. Enjoy what you've got and reach for what you want and the process ends up mattering the most.

stronger. Barry's death is something I can never fix or undo. All I can do is honor him and try to bring some meaning to something that was so horrible.

My first concern was getting justice for Barry, so I aligned with some wonderful LGBT and outsider legal agencies and support networks. We went to trial and got as much justice as we could. We were able to get an apology from President Clinton for "don't ask, don't tell," which we felt contributed to an air of permissibility for that kind of hatred. I've raised money for charity. I've spoken out, and I've tried to support other trans women. I say yes. I show up. And I do what I can.

I went for many years without speaking a word to Mom, and then we both tentatively reached out. Now we call and just talk and text and laugh. And so now at forty-seven I can enjoy that mother-daughter relationship I always dreamt of having. You have to walk through the fire to get stronger. ◼

John Duran

I'm John Duran. I am currently Mayor of the city of West Hollywood, California, and have served on the City Council for eighteen years. Voters elect council members to four-year terms. Then the mayor's job rotates each spring among the five council members. During my time on the council I've been mayor five times. I am proud to say that I am one of the longest-serving LGBT elected officials—and the first Latino LGBT elected official—in the country.

I'm also an attorney. I started out as a civil rights lawyer during the HIV/AIDS epidemic in the 1980s. I went on to do LGBT rights work in the '90s, before being elected to office in 2001.

I was born to a lower middle-class Latino family on the east side of Los Angeles. I survived twelve years of Catholic grade school and high school. Then I went on to college and law school.

Believe that

you are

enough

and you

can do it.

Take that

deep

breath

and

walk forward

with the

fear and

anxiety,

but

don't let

them

stop you.

I was supposed to be a corporate lawyer. My life took a dramatic turn when AIDS hit in the mid-1980s. I'm one of four HIV-positive elected officials in the country. I almost died several times in the mid-1990s. I've put back forty pounds, and I'm doing great today thanks to the miracle drugs that came along.

I lost more than 100 friends from 1985 to 1995. These years have been seared into my consciousness. I think that a lot of the women and men who responded to the crisis suffer from PTSD. We were in our twenties and thirties, and life had not given us the tools to process more than 100 deaths in ten years. I think the hardest thing was to lose two law partners, my roommates, and some of my closest allies in the cause. Even when I made new friends, we'd celebrate a victory and he was soon dying—she'd make some progress and then she would die. It was a very rough period.

I suffered from severe challenges with alcoholism and drug addiction. I couldn't believe that God existed, given how traumatic my world was. I knew I had to find a higher power. Although it was difficult for me, I sobered up twenty-two years ago. I practiced the twelve-step program and went back to church. I found a way back to a spiritual center that's helped me put all these things in their proper place.

During my life as a gay man and an LGBT rights lawyer, my family's been great. My mom passed away earlier this year, but she and my dad were some of the first members of Parents and Friends of Lesbians and Gays, in the 1980s. They became champions for the gay community. My mom also was a school board member here in Los Angeles. And so politics ran through her blood to me.

During the AIDS epidemic, we didn't have much choice. People were dying, suffering horrible deaths. There was nothing I could do other than walk through it and say goodbye over 100 times. As I look back at that terrible time, I know that today I am enough and I can do it. At this point, nothing's going to scare me. Nothing's going to intimidate me. I take a deep breath and move forward—with the fear and anxiety—but not letting them stop me.

I know life is short, life is fragile. I know every moment counts. And I know at some point it's terminal. So living with that perspective gives me an advantage because not much rocks my boat. ∎

SAFE AND FREE

Do I do everything right?
Of course not,
but my heart is open
and so are my eyes.

My name is John Anthony D'Amico.

I am the second son and youngest child of lower middle-class parents. They did their best. My father was a World War II and Korean War veteran; my mother was a liberated, stay-at-home warrior. They raised four children, who all succeed in immeasurable ways, in a world that was ultimately unrecognizable to my parents by the end of their lives.

I grew up. Gay. I was a gay ten-year-old if ever there was one. Looking at old photos of myself, I know that; I "came out" at seventeen, but I was always gay. I certainly don't remember not feeling gay.

I went to Art School as an undergraduate. I was a knuckle-headed kid who thought he knew everything.

I learned I am HIV positive in 1988. At the LA Free Clinic. At that time people with HIV lived as best they could, but mostly died of AIDS. I still have the carbon copy of the test result page. It was printed on a dot-matrix printer. Reactive.

That was more than thirty years ago.

I went to Graduate School in Architecture in 1988.

I met my husband in 1992. I invited myself to his birthday party. I brought him a box of instant hash browns wrapped in brown paper as a gift. It worked. We're still in love.

I work hard. I've worked at UCLA managing new building construction projects since 2001.

I went to Graduate School again in 2008 for a second graduate degree in Aesthetics and Politics.

I am political. I am the Mayor Pro Tempore of the city of West Hollywood and will be Mayor in 2019 if reelected. I was first elected in 2011.

Both of those jobs are incredibly satisfying and I love them. I understand the value of commitment, education, and patience. Life continues to surprise me at fifty-five.

I guess you might say I didn't want to be erased. ■

Andrea James

My name is Andrea James. I do a lot of political media, mostly in support of transgender rights—involving film, television, and any other media that can help create the change we're after. We've survived plenty of terrible things over the years, and my work today is focused on changing the conversation a bit.

I just did a film for Showtime about a friend and his husband who adopted a child. There are states where gays cannot adopt children. And so I wanted to do a piece about that because I was adopted. I wanted to pay it forward. There are 400,000 children in foster care, and there are all these great gay, lesbian, bi, and trans couples who would be great parents.

I grew up in the Midwest—Illinois—and lived on a farm for a while, where we grew sweet corn, watermelons, and popcorn. Then we moved to Indiana where I went to middle school and high school. I was adopted and have a sibling who was also adopted. I left Indiana to go to graduate school in Chicago. I was there for about ten years working in advertising, and while I was there I did my gender transition.

Kids start to form their gender identity between three and six. And before the Internet it was very hard to find information. So one of the first projects I did was to write a website that's like *Our Bodies, Ourselves* for trans people. I wanted to write what I wish I would have found when I was ten and went to the local library.

It was certainly a challenge for me because there's so much pressure to conform to gender stereotypes and gender roles. There were times I experienced such bullying that I stopped expressing myself for a long time just to feel safe. I was in about seventh grade. I think a lot of trans people reach that moment when they don't express themselves anymore. And then finally they reach a point where they can't stand it and eventually transition.

And when I transitioned it was still very much for personal safety. Plus, to get and keep a job you needed to make a sharp distinction and be very feminine. So I'm very glad that now people can be more genderqueer and more fluid in their presentation.

I transitioned when I was in my midtwenties and finished all the physical aspects at around thirty. Before that I created a gender hell of my own making. I proclaimed, "You want me to be masculine? Okay, I will do all of it." I went to an all-male college, which is hard to find. I wrote beer commercials for many years. I was very good at it. But eventually I said to myself, "What am I doing?"

I was very careful at work. It was a very masculine environment. I thought I might get fired. And luckily I was not. But then a friend of mine was dating a guy who was murdered. It became a big story about "don't ask, don't tell" because he was in the military and beaten to death on a Fourth of July weekend by his unit mates. I saw how my friend was treated in the media. She was transgender, and I thought why am I selling hamburgers and beer and cereal when friends are being treated this way? So she and I came out here and started doing film and television work with the goal of improving how trans people are depicted in the media. The end game of the trans movement is for everybody to feel they can express and identify themselves in a way that feels free.

I think one of the critical turning points for me was when I let those people break me in seventh grade, when I let them change who I was, or at least how I expressed it outwardly. I let go of my self-esteem and self-love. And so what I've been trying to do ever since is to get back to a place where I love myself. And it's not easy. They say hurt people hurt people, and there are a lot of hurt people. I've had some very unpleasant experiences with stalkers, harassers, and haters. Overcoming that and not letting that get to you is really what I try to do. I try to focus on the things that are important and not dwell on the past or reinvent the future. I try to be a little more present. ■

People
will try to
break you, but
you can use love
to bend them
to your will.
So it's really been
a great journey—
one that has
taught me to be
a better person
and to meet
people
where they are.

We have to continue fighting for our rights to be who we are and want to be. The discrimination toward us is unacceptable.

My name is Karina Samala. I serve as chair of the Los Angeles Human Relations Commission Transgender Advisory Council. I'm also a member of the West Hollywood Transgender Advisory Board. These advisory groups help city officials develop policy on matters relating to the transgender community, such as employment, housing, health care, education, equal rights, and hate crimes prevention.

I was born in the Philippines, the only biological male sibling in a family with seven girls. My parents had been hoping for a son to carry on the family name. As young as six, though, I felt different. I would dress in my sisters' clothing. I knew I was a female inside.

My mother's family was Seventh Day Adventist, and I attended a Seventh Day Adventist school. It was very strict. My parents died early in my life, and my sisters raised me. They knew about my sexual identity. They watched over me, even hiring someone to take me to school. They nurtured me and helped me develop. So my childhood was really wonderful.

When I finished college and graduate school, I went to work for a major defense contractor. There I began to face a challenge that would tear me apart inside and eventually lead me to the activism I practice today. The turning point came when I was assigned to work on government-funded projects related to satellites and missile systems. My work required that I have a top-secret clearance. So I had to undergo extensive background checks that included questions about my sexual orientation: Are you a homosexual? If I answered yes, I could lose my security clearance and possibly my job. The fear was that you could be blackmailed and the nation's defense systems I was working on could be compromised. I had to lie because they would never give me my clearance if I told the truth.

While I kept my secret at work, I got involved with a gay bowling league in Long Beach. Some of my bowling team members urged me to compete in the annual Closet Ball pageant sponsored by the Imperial Court of Los Angeles and Hollywood. In the competition I would dress first as a male and then return dressed and made up as a woman. I won the competition as a girl and started to compete in other pageants and fundraising events that benefited the transgender community.

By night I was a transgender beauty queen and by day a senior engineer at a major defense contractor. So I was

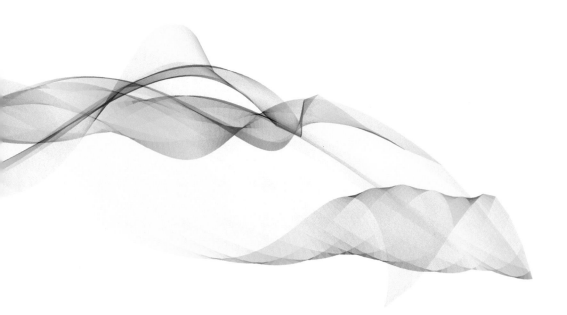

living this double life. I was not happy.

I eventually found a mentor who was a former West Hollywood council member. He was developing an advisory group on LGBT issues to work with the Los Angeles County Sheriff Department. He invited me to join the group. I was then asked to help advise LAPD on similar issues. I found myself out on the streets with officers working with the gay and transgender community, helping to develop policies that would guide law enforcement's interactions with LGBT people.

But I was torn inside. I had a job that paid lots of money but knew I could not continue living a double life. I then quit my job so that I could be myself twenty-four seven.

I've always been a fighter. I fight back when members of my community are threatened. They come to me for help—with family problems, boyfriend, and girlfriend problems. If they get in trouble with the law, I go to the station with them. I visit the jails and try to work to solve problems there.

In recent years, I've been recognized for my continuing work to assure equal rights and human rights for transgenders. I was the recipient of the Lifetime Achievement and Stonewall 40 Trans-Heroes awards from the International Court Council and the Martin Luther King "Keeper of the Dream" and Rainbow Key awards from the city of West Hollywood. A few years ago, the city of Los Angeles chose me to receive a Spirit of Los Angeles tribute. I'm humbled by all the attention, but I realize that much remains to be done.

As new and evolving sexual identity and freedom issues come to the fore, it's going to be mandatory for city officials and employees to receive transgender sensitivity training. We have to continue fighting for our rights to be who we are and want to be—especially for the young people of our community and future generations. We need to fight back. The discrimination toward us is unacceptable. ■

Lorri Jean

I'm the CEO of the Los Angeles LGBT Center and have held the job, with one short break, since 1993. That makes me the longest-tenured leader of an LGBT organization in the movement. I see the steel in these photos as a metaphor for what it takes to be a leader. You must be strong. You must be unyielding, but you must also be able to bend.

I grew up in Arizona. My folks were farmers, and I was the eldest of their three kids. When you grow up on a farm and you're a girl and you're the oldest child, you are given all kinds of responsibility, irrespective of gender roles. My parents raised me to have a very strong self-concept, which has been the key to my happiness and my success in life.

My dad had been a hard-scrabble farmer and never made any money. He eventually began to enjoy some success raising pigs. But when I was in eighth grade, disease spread among the herd. At that time the federal government had a deal to pay farmers to kill the herd and eradicate the disease, splitting the cost with the state. But the state wouldn't pay its share, and we lost the family farm.

I decided that was so wrong. I wanted to be a lawyer and I was going to fix things that were wrong. After I graduated from Arizona State, I went east to go to law school.

I also faced the more personal challenge of deciding as a young adult whether I was going to live my life being open and honest about my sexual orientation. I first thought that I had to hide it. I wanted to be a lawyer. I wanted to run for office and make the world a better place. I thought that coming out would screw up my plans. And I wondered if my folks would reject me.

If you want to be happy, tell other people the truth…

After realizing I was a lesbian, it took me about two weeks to also realize that I could not hide this from my family. It took me some months, though, before I told my mom and her first request was, "Please don't go on TV about this, and please don't tell your father because he'll blame me." But that only lasted for a little while.

I got my first job as an attorney in Washington, DC, without disclosing my sexual orientation. I talked to other lawyers in town who were older than I about whether I should come out, and they all told me no, don't do it. But I was young

and naive—and there are lots of benefits to being young and naive. And so I decided I would come out. I knew I could lose my job because I was working for a federal agency and had a top-secret and higher security clearance. And back then they took security clearances away from gay people because they thought that we were at risk for blackmail. I decided I was going to test that. I was going to tell the head of my agency, who was a Reagan appointee, a sixty-three-year-old black man who had been a three star general

in the army—not exactly the profile of someone you think would be happy to have an open lesbian on his team.

And then the police raided a gay bar in Washington wearing masks and gloves. It was in the early days of the AIDS epidemic. I soon found myself organizing a demonstration on the steps of the Washington, DC, police department. And I was on the news that night and on the front page of the *Washington Post* the next day.

All the publicity foiled my

plan to tell my bosses about my sexual orientation. So when I walked into the agency the next day nobody would look at me, nobody would talk to me. And as I went into my office, I thought, "I really misjudged this—this is going to be a challenge."

I closed my door. In about a half hour I heard a banging on my door. It was the head of the agency—that same general. He stood in my door and said at full volume so everybody could hear, "I saw you on TV last night and read about you in the paper this morning." A pause followed as my career flashed before my eyes. "I just wanted you to know, I don't want you to be sitting here afraid that you're going to lose your security clearance and your job because it's clear that you're open about who you are. And I just want you to know I'm proud that you're a member of our family." Well, everybody heard him and that gave them permission to be supportive. I had misjudged him. So it was a good lesson: never paint people with a single brush.

What's helped me respond to all the challenges? I was somewhat naive when I was young, but I was self-confident at the same time. The response I received from family members and colleagues was determined, in some ways, by how confident I was. I am an eternal optimist. My life had worked for me no matter the challenges. I had been happy. I had been loved, and I believed that would continue.

Have the courage of your convictions. The most powerful choice any of us can make is to be true to ourselves, whether that's professionally or personally. ■

...and, more importantly, tell yourself the truth.

Frank DeCaro

My name is Frank DeCaro. I am a stand-up comedian *and* a journalist *and* an author. *Let me see…anything else?* That's enough.

I'm Italian Catholic and an only child from New Jersey. I like to say I grew up eighteen miles and a world away from New York City.

I was a very good student, but I got picked on a lot. I was very gay even if I didn't yet have that word in my vocabulary.

My life changed when I came out of the closet at sixteen. At about the same time, I got a role in the senior play, *Bye Bye Birdie*. I played Paul Lynde's part, the father, Harry MacAfee.

I was out as a gay person, and I was making people laugh for the first time. I wanted to keep doing this.

I was dead set on making a life of my own that was more like what I saw on television than what I was used to. And when I realized I was gay, I was like, "This is even better. I'm even more different than they are. I'm not them."

So I was this kid from the suburbs who wanted to be a star. My parents didn't know what to make of it. I came from very humble roots. You were not really encouraged to stand out or to dream big. I had to constantly challenge myself to believe that I could make it. I was really driven to better myself. When I got in

Get out there and live!

to Northwestern University, there was no turning back. I saw people traveling, going to the theater, eating exotic foods at beautiful restaurants, and wearing fashionable clothes. I was like, "I'm doing this."

But if you were gay you had to surmount other obstacles, some subtle, others blatant. Only a few years before I became the first openly gay newspaper columnist, I was asked by a hiring editor when I went for a fashion writing job how I felt about the "faggot" factor: "Everyone's gonna think you're gay." When I wrote my first column, I started off without hesitation writing "I'm a gay guy and …"

My column was a hit and led to my first book, a memoir called *A Boy Named Phyllis*. I'm now working on my fifth book about drag in show business, coming out soon from Rizzoli.

I was fearless when I was younger and relished my suc-cess. When I was in my forties, fear showed up. And once my mother was gone, I think that's when doubt started to set in too. My father would always say, "When is your bubble going to burst?" And it was the year my mother died, 2003.

That year was the worst. *The Daily Show* didn't renew my contract, and a very lucrative writing gig that I'd had for years fell through. So I had no job, no mother, and didn't know what I was going to do next. I had to build my way back.

I reinvented myself as a radio personality on SiriusXM. Although we did some really great things over twelve years, I can't say I was happy for most of them.

I was turning fifty and my friend Lisa Lampanelli, in a kind of intervention, said to me, "You've got to get your life together." I thought, "She's right. I've got to shake things up."

I lost 105 pounds, which was great. And my husband and I decided if our rent in New York City goes to where we think it's going to go, we're going to move. And it did, and we did.

We moved to LA about five years ago. I enjoy LA every day. I go on the road with Lisa a lot, playing large venues and small. Making three thousand people laugh at something is quite powerful. It feels really good.

There are these lines from *Auntie Mame* that come to mind when I am feeling a bit overwhelmed: "Life is a banquet and most poor suckers are starving to death," and "Live, Agnes, live." Even though I think it's a total cliché for a gay guy to be quoting *Auntie Mame*, I think that's the truth of the matter.

Of course, she ends up pregnant, and I'm glad that never happened to me. ∎

John Heilman

My name is John Heilman. I'm a law school professor in Los Angeles and have been for thirty years. I am also an elected member of the West Hollywood City Council.

I grew up in Cleveland, Ohio. My parents were divorced when I was very young. My brother and I lived with our mother. She was intelligent and kind. She treated people fairly. But her need for alcohol took precedence over a lot in her life. When she died I reflected on a life that had been lost in many respects: she had many abilities that we're not fulfilled.

Growing up in an unstable household made me feel anxious and insecure. I was afraid to be on elevators. I was afraid to be in certain places where I felt like I could be trapped. None of my fears were rooted in reality, of course, but for me they felt real enough.

So I needed to find a way out.

My salvation was school. I

Be productive and be kind. And don't forget to dance. And laugh.

did well and that became my ticket. I went to Northwestern and pretty much never went back. After college, I took a year off and then went to law school at USC. That's what brought me to Southern California.

People who have anxieties don't suddenly get rid of them. They carry the anxieties with them. Even successful law professors and city councilmen. Mine traveled along with me from Cleveland years ago. The fears come and go.

As you get older you recognize them; you realize they don't have to define you. I think to some degree they make you care about your performance in the classroom and at work—even keep you on your toes.

I've taught for thirty years, but I still go into a class and worry whether I am I going to do okay. Am I going to mess something up in class? I worry

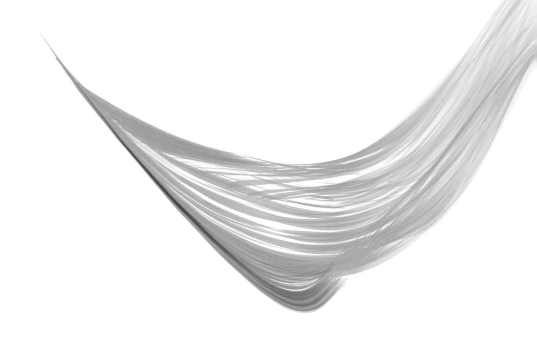

about doing a good job, making sure I'm explaining topics clearly. It's no different from serving on the City Council. Every year we face a new set of issues and challenges. And I always try to do the best job not only for the current residents, but also for the people who will be in the city in the future.

When I was growing up in Cleveland, I felt different as a gay person, and I was treated differently because of it. Even when I was a little older and in law school, I still felt the sense that I was different. Of course, it was a much different time then. Many firms didn't hire openly gay associates. Now, all the big firms hire gay people. In fact, many firms make an extra effort to ensure they have a diverse workplace. But that wasn't the case when I graduated. It was challenging.

I sometimes marvel at my journey through life. I've had so many wonderful opportunities. I've learned so much and I continue to learn new things every day. As a teacher, I've met so many amazing people from all over the world. Today, I try to approach life by working hard and having some fun along the way. I like to laugh at myself and laugh at the human condition. But I always try to serve others. And I always try to make things better. ■

TRANSITION

I am an actor, writer, and improviser. Since I came to LA almost twenty years ago, I've done a lot of TV and live performing—a little bit of everything.

I grew up in North Carolina. I was part of a lovely family, but mine was a pretty conservative, southern upbringing. And I was in and out of hospitals a lot during the first two or three years of my life. Facing down those health problems made me feel like a fighter. I knew, too, that I was different from other people. I was gay.

I had two different lives—my life with family and the alternative reality I created for myself. I was told that creatively there's no one like you. I suppose that's one of my greatest assets. It also meant then that I didn't fit in. I was told that it would be very hard for me to find a partner or to work with creative collaborators.

I walled myself off from people. It's been a journey to open myself and be vulnerable with other people. I've had to make all my own stuff and forge my own connections.

But the biggest obstacle I've had to overcome is to get out of my own way and not listen to people who say it will be too hard and I should try to do something else. I really never considered giving up as an actor and creative performer. There was nothing else I wanted to do with my life.

I came from a Presbyterian family who didn't talk about a lot of things. I assumed for a really long time that my family wouldn't be okay with me being gay. But they've been very accepting and loving. I've learned to open up to them and share with them. I think my own hang-ups got in the way. When I did a one-man show in New York, they came up and saw me perform.

I also have a great community of people now whom I work with to create some really crazy intimate shows, legit theater, and bigger splashier things. I have, indeed, found wonderful collaborators who make my work even better.

What I tell myself is one foot in front of the other, one step at a time. ■

Embrace the difficulties, hold on and it will all be fine.

Sherry Vine

Hi, Sherry Vine here. I am an actor and performer in drag. A drag queen.

I grew up outside of Baltimore, Maryland, and I've been acting and performing since I was three. It's all I've ever done.

My parents back then were like hippies, without the drugs. They were a little too old to be part of the drug movement, but they were into the music. They were very liberal and cool: "Oh, you're dating someone black, great; you're gay, whatever."

Overcoming obstacles in my life has been an evolutionary process. Many years ago my sister passed away. That was a big moment. You never really recover from that.

It's a process of peeling off layers to be your authentic self.

When I started doing drag it was—and continues to be—a learning experience. I felt empowered when I performed. It's like wearing a mask that gives you this freedom. And when I took it off I felt I lost it. After doing it for so long I've learned to integrate that feeling of freedom in my everyday life, even without that mask.

Most obstacles are self-imposed—things that you put on yourself. And one of the few things I like about getting older is you start peeling those layers away like an onion. "Why do I give a shit about this? Who cares? This is stupid." Something you believed was so important five years ago is now unimportant. It's like, "Who cares?"

I'm an actor and Sherry is a character in the same way that Elvira is a character or Pee-wee Herman. I don't lead two lives. I'm Keith during my daily life. But everything I do, every minute of the day, is some way connected to the show. I'm going to the gym to stay fit; I'm writing new material; I'm rehearsing. I'm working a lot. My whole life is about performing. But Sherry is a character. When I come off stage and I take this off, she's done. I'm Keith. That's the real person.

When I first started performing as Sherry and I was working almost every night, there came a time when I would look in the mirror and see long platinum hair and no eyebrows. I wondered where's Keith? I know that I'm not trans and I'm a man. So I cut my hair and I let my eyebrows grow back. I found a nice middle ground where I liked the way I looked in drag and the way I looked out of drag as a man—a big gay guy, but a man.

And so I've found that balance in my life. Everybody has to work to be happy, right? It may not be hard labor but it's a process. That's what I mean by having to strip things away. That may mean that if the scales have tipped and Person X in my life causes me more anxiety than pleasure, they have to go. I'm constantly in the process of doing that.

I used to be a person who would freak out if my flight was canceled. I was up there at the counter screaming. I decided that this is not helping; this won't change anything. And so now I'm like, "Okay, maybe that's a sign that I need to sit here for an hour and drink this coffee, write, or read this magazine." So letting go is a constant work in progress.

I'm doing what I'm supposed to be doing and I'm happy. You have to be happy no matter how much work it may take because that's all we really have. ■

Eugene Maysky

I'm Eugene Maysky. I'm from Russia where I lived and worked until I made the decision to move to Los Angeles. Here I work at a fine jewelry company and as a stringer for a Russian movie website. I also volunteer with the Midnight Stroll outreach program that involves LGBTQ volunteers in stepping out into the night to provide, food, water, socks, and blankets to the homeless.

I grew up in St. Petersburg—one of the most beautiful cities in the world.

But there was a problem. Being gay in Russia could present a threat to your existence. I'm just not talking about a lot of people being mistreated; I'm also talking about some people ending up in their graves.

It's important to
gay-it-forward.
Tell someone who
needs to hear it,
"You are not alone;
there are people
who love you
and accept you
just the way
you are."

LOVE IS LOVE

I grew up in the media in Russia. I was on the radio since I was eight and on TV since I was a teenager. I worked as a presenter, a radio DJ, and later a producer. I thought that if I worked hard enough and if I didn't tell anybody my secret, people would like me for who I am as a person. But I realized that it didn't matter how much positive energy I put out there trying to entertain people and make them happy, it would always come down to the fact that nobody would let me work and live as I wanted because I was gay.

I experienced situations that frightened me. And I decided at some point you had to choose how you're going to live your life. Are you going to be able to be with your tribe? Are you going to be who you really are and live free and not look over your shoulder every time you go home?

I took one suitcase and flew fifteen hours over the ocean to start a new life in LA at forty-one. I just didn't want to be afraid anymore.

I haven't seen my family for two years. It's tough because I love my family and I miss them terribly. My mom cried for three years when I told her I was gay. She thought, "Oh my God, somebody's going to kill him or hurt him or he's going to get some horrible disease and die." Even though we've been apart for a long time, I think she feels better knowing that I am safe.

When I think about how I've overcome the obstacles in my life, I think about a boy or girl who feels she is totally alone. She thinks she has no one to talk to; he doesn't know where to get help or how to survive a turbulent time in his life.

It's so very important to let them know they are not alone. There are people who will accept and love them just the way they are. There are people who are working to make their lives better. It's important to be there for them because I think if somebody would have told me that when I was a kid in Russia, it would have made me very happy. ■

Aaron Barrera aka Chacha

Life's too short. Don't waste it. Live it. Enjoy it. Love it.

I'm Aaron Barrera. When I dress in drag I go by Chacha. During the day I'm Aaron.

Growing up I knew there was nothing wrong with me. I was born as the person I was supposed to be. I knew I should allow myself to be that person and not be ashamed. That's the trick about this whole thing—dealing with the shame others create around you.

And getting through that was difficult.

I grew up in Mexico. My father was from Spain. My mother was Native American. My parents both worked constantly so I was left alone a lot at home. That's when I started developing characters. Salesmen would knock on the door, and I would tell them, "I can't talk now but my twin will see you."

So I would leave the room and go put on a pair of glasses, change my shirt and come out. And they'd look at me and say, "Kid, you just went back there and changed your shirt." But to me it was another character.

Coming out to my family as a gay man, as a drag queen, was difficult. But my own internal voice was always telling me, "It's okay, it's okay, you're good. Just try it. Just do it."

And I would say, "You're crazy; I'm not doing it."

My mother and sister, who had died suddenly, never became the women they wanted to be. They we're frustrated their whole lives. I didn't want that to happen to me. Life is too short. You can lose it in a second.

I finally found the courage to listen to that voice inside me. I

wanted to live. I wasn't afraid of dying anymore. I moved to New York to pursue acting. And that's when Chacha was born. I was free to be myself and free to let that little boy's experiment take flight.

For me doing drag is always about letting my alter ego take over. I give that person the freedom to do whatever she wants to do. I'm on the passenger side and that person's driving. She knows where she's going and I just let her be. I know that when she comes back home and takes everything off, then she becomes me again.

Chacha is my other me. ■

Always Be
Different!!!

Dr. Mimi

I am Doctor Mimi Hoang.

I'm a Staff Psychologist with Loyola Marymount University's Student Psychological Services. I also teach at Antioch University within the Master's in Clinical Psychology program, which includes the nation's first LGBT Specialization. And then on the side I offer consulting, training and continuing education around diversity issues for professionals and the general public. I've also had nearly twenty years of LGBTQ community leadership, including co-founding three bisexual organizations in Los Angeles (Los Angeles Bi Task Force; amBi: LA's Bisexual Social Community; and Fluid at UCLA). I wear a lot of hats.

I'm mixed Chinese and Vietnamese, and born in Vietnam. My parents fled the country with me after the Vietnam War when I was very young. We came here as refugees. And I grew up with very little exposure to LGBT identity, culture, and community.

Be honest with yourself because that's where your strength and your superpower come from.

Coming out was probably one of the greatest challenges I've had to overcome in my life. Growing up as an immigrant and ethnic minority was challenging enough. But then I also began to realize that I was different in this other way. I struggled to figure out who I was. I knew I didn't quite identify as gay, but I didn't identify as straight either. It wasn't until I got to college that I heard the term *bisexual* for the first time, and it dawned on me that maybe that's who I am. I didn't have role models, and I didn't even know what questions to ask. I had no concept of what it meant not to be straight and not to be gay either. So there was no clear path for me that I could see. And growing up in a very traditional Asian-American family, I knew the topic was taboo. It was very hard.

While I was enrolled in college, I worked with both a therapist and a mentor who helped me understand and accept who I was. I learned to be honest with myself. I also had some very supportive friends who were there for me when I first came out. And so that's how my activism started. I wanted to help build a community so that it wouldn't be so hard for other people to come out.

Coming out to my mom and dad was difficult. My parents had very little knowledge or awareness about the issue. They knew only the negative stereotypes about someone who is queer, someone who's bisexual. So it's taken a lot of time. But they're in a much better place now.

I live in Los Angeles, which is a

very liberal area, but there are pockets and groups who think bisexuality is abnormal or believe negative stereotypes. Before I became more of a public activist, I was labeled as confused because the assumption is you're either gay or you're straight. And if you're not one or the other, you have to figure it out. I've had both men and women say that they won't date me because of my orientation. Some men will fetishize it. They have a certain fan-tasy about what a bisexual woman is like. They don't take bisexuality seriously. They try to make it into something that's fun for them, assuming that we bisexual women are open to any kind of sex with anybody. That's hard because, even though it seems like it's accepting, it's an objectification.

Co-founding Fluid, amBi, and the Los Angeles Bi Task Force has taken lots of blood, sweat, and tears because of continued biphobia and bi erasure, but being able to attend the first Bisexual Community Roundtable at the White House in 2013 felt like a phenomenal accomplishment. I continue to educate people every day wearing my many hats because there are serious health disparities facing my community that we cannot ignore.

And today there is an ever-broader spectrum between gay and straight. People are identifying as bisexual, pansexual, queer, fluid, and omni. I think bisexuality is beautiful. I consider it a blessing for me to be able to experience love with men, women, other genders. The most important thing is to be yourself. ■

Alaska Thunderfuck

My name is Alaska, like the state. My full name is Alaska Thunderfuck 5000. When I return home from a trip out of the country and I have to write down my occupation, I always write "artist" because it sounds fancy. But when they ask me, I say, "I dress up like a lady and sing songs."

I do drag.

I grew up in Erie, Pennsylvania. We lived by the airport and the railroad tracks. We were poor, but everyone was poor so I didn't know the difference. I have two brothers and an older sister. My family loves to laugh. My mom is so hilarious and strong, and she knows how to swear really well. It's like poetry.

Growing up I didn't know any queer people, and I hadn't seen any films or television that represented who I was. I didn't know who I was for a long time. I think that's a struggle that all young people go through. But it's especially hard when you're a queer kid, and you don't know what you're supposed to do.

I'm still figuring it out. But now I'm blessed to be part of a community that is supportive, amazing, and cool; we interact and show each other the way and figure it out together. I'm so grateful for this crazy ridiculous thing that I do for a living. Mom and Dad watch everything that I'm in, and they cheer right along. Even my uncles, as bro-ish and dude-like as they are, are strangely supportive. But there's always the question of how long will it last. When it's not a thing anymore, then what? But I hope that I get to be ninety and they prop me up in the doorway, and I can still croak out a song on stage.

I think my mom is probably the strongest person I've ever seen. If I inherited a fraction of her interior strength, that would be amazing. I mean I'm just really grateful to have her in my life. And the people who did drag before us show me every day who I want to be, who I would strive to be.

People ask me, "And when you're not doing drag, who are you?" Well, my mom calls me Justin and my family calls me Justin. But I can't hide very easily from my fans; as soon I open my mouth they know exactly who I am—Alaska. And I'm like six-foot-one in my bare feet, so I'm this giant alien person who really can't hide. But I don't like to draw attention to myself and make a fuss when I'm not in drag.

Experience has been my best teacher. You have to go toward the stuff that you're afraid of. The closer you get to it, you realize that it's just a veil; it's just ether, and it's not real. And that's where growth happens—especially for an artist. Don't be afraid of facing that fear, dying that death over and over again. ■

If you're pushing yourself to places you're afraid of, places you're uncomfortable going, places you haven't tried before, that's how you're going to grow and learn.

STRONG

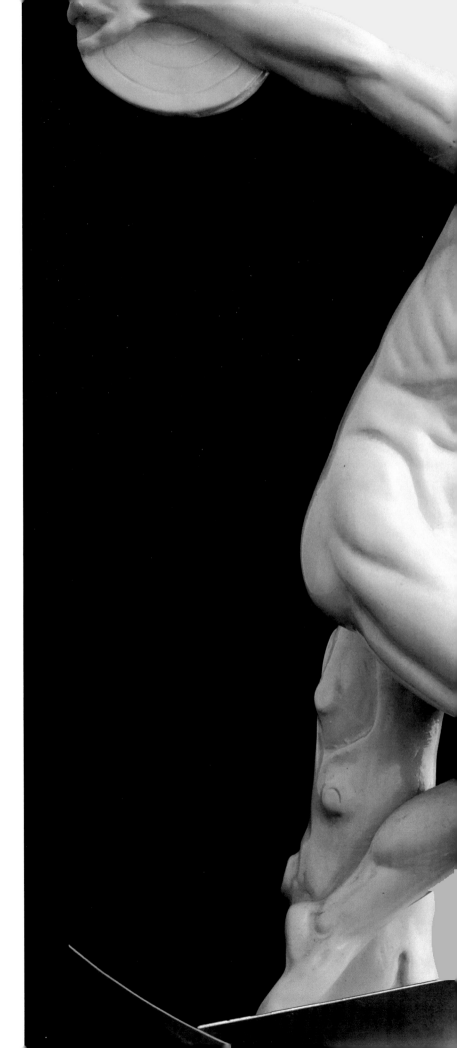

Regina Cates

I'm Regina Victoria Cates, a writer and author. I am a spiritual teacher and superhero.

I earned a master's degree in leadership and I used to have a traditional job—the regular nine-to-five stuff. I enjoyed it, but I got really bored with it.

My mission today is to spread inspiration and positivity through my organization Romancing Your Soul, the books and articles I write, my podcasts, videos, and courses. I'm dedicated to letting everybody in the world know we are worthy and we should be seen as the individuals we are.

I came into this life with steel-like armor that allowed me to endure the abuse I felt growing up in the 1960s as a member of a fundamentalist church in the southern United States. I knew I was gay around age four or five. When you're forced to go to church constantly and hear how horrible you are and how you're going to spend all eternity with Satan that in itself is hell enough.

At age eighteen I could no longer contain my big secret, and I finally confessed to being gay. Yes, my worst nightmare did come true. I was sent to a physician who sexually molested me. Then I was locked in a psychiatric hospital because they thought I was depressed. Sure, I was depressed: I had just been sexually violated. And my parents and religion wanted to change me.

My parents then sent me to a psychiatrist who told them he would never be able to change my sexuality because I was born this way. I felt validation for the first time in my life.

I was very fortunate because there has always been an obstinate person in me who said, "No, this isn't right." I knew early in life that some original creative source made each of us unique. I felt something deep within me that is connected to everything that's alive. And it gave me the power to say I'm not going to take this. My belief that we are more than what we can touch and feel helped save my life.

You don't have to be religious to tap into a deep spirituality. I work with people all over the world to help them look inside themselves to discover why they are unhappy and what's keeping them from being okay with who they are. To give thanks for the magnificent gift of life, I believed we must express our uniqueness.

I think whenever we can share who we really are, instead of the stereotype of who people think we are, we are making connections. Whenever we can share, for example, that LGBTQ people are ordinary everyday people from many different walks of life and our goal is to love and be loved, we are serving a powerful truth that will destroy divisive stereotypes. I think LGBTQ people who have felt so much rejection in their lives know how to accept others. They've gone through pain so they know what it's like to cause pain to someone else, and they want to avoid that.

I think we build the capacity to be empathetic through enduring hard times. Whether you're a cancer survivor or the CEO of a corporation who succeeds against all odds, when you tap into your capacity to empathize with others, you're able to truly change the world.

We are all connected. ■

When we view
the challenges of life
as opportunities
to grow,
we blossom.

Maya Angelou said nobody is born great.

Martin Luther King had greatness thrust upon him. He knew what to do with it.

When it happens you take it and respond to it in the best way you can.

My name is Jon Imparato. I'm the artistic director of The Lily Tomlin/Jane Wagner Cultural Arts Center, which is a major program of the Los Angeles LGBT Center. I produce and direct theater, comedy, special events, and fundraisers for the Center.

I grew up in Brooklyn and Long Island in a lower middle-class Italian family. I remember a wonderful life—but it included both great joy and great pain. In 1963 being pegged as a gay kid in school was not easy. I was beaten up and called a "faggot" and "queer." I didn't want anyone to call me a sissy boy because that might actually be who I was, something that I had hidden in my heart.

But I was born with a naturally gregarious personality, and I was always funny. When I was in the sixth grade, my teacher said to me, "I want you to get up and tell jokes at the end of class on Friday." He gave me a joke book, and I thought that if I could make people laugh, they will laugh with me, not at me. And that would make me cool.

And then that same teacher asked if I wanted to play Doctor Kildare in this little skit about the benefits of using dental floss. I went on stage, feeling the floorboards under my feet and the lights on me. I couldn't see them, but they could see me. And I made them laugh.

I went, "Okay, I'm home. This is it." I ran home and told my family that I'm going to be an actor. They didn't know what I was talking about. They thought I was crazy.

My parents came to a parent-teacher night, which was a rarity for them. I was demonstrating the pottery wheel as part of my art class. When we got in the car, I thought that I'm going to get the shit kicked out of me because they found out how bad a student I was. My mother told me that they had an interesting conversation with the teacher. And I asked what happened. And she said, "Well, he said that you're an artist and you'll always be an artist and that if you get Cs, that's probably the best you're going to do. And to lay off." And I sat in the back of the car thinking, "I'm an artist. I love being called an artist. That feels so great. I'm an artist. I'm not a painter."

When I came out to my family, it was very hard. I didn't speak to my parents for almost nine months. I wanted them to know that I could live without them and survive without them. The estrangement was driving them crazy and driving me crazy. So I went to visit my sister who was living with my parents. She said, "You're driving me crazy. They're driving me crazy. You work it out."

Then she left. We all cried and my mother said, "I had no idea." I'm like, "No idea? I begged you for the six-album Judy Garland box set for my tenth birthday. What do you mean you had no idea?" My mother is gone now, but my family has been incredibly supportive.

My greatest challenge that I had to overcome was inside of me—a dreaded fear that I was abnormal and something was wrong with me. I would go to church and pray for hours as a ten-year-old kid. I had no language for what it was, but I'd say, "God don't make me be different." I wouldn't use the word. I thought I might have a life of persecution, or I'd have to become a priest to hide it, and my attraction for boys was unhealthy and unnatural. I had a deep need for faith, and

I thought God was punishing me. I experienced confusion and self-hatred. I knew there was goodness in me, but the gay thing meant I was messed up or diseased or something was wrong. So wrestling that demon meant coming to terms with how I could be gay and still be a good person and have a good life.

I wanted to have kids, too. I couldn't get married and have children then. But somebody told me when I was nineteen that I had to learn to let dreams fall away so a new dream can come true. I fell in love with this amazing man. It didn't matter so much whether I had a kid. I wanted to be in love with somebody, and I was in love with somebody who was wonderful. So I said to myself, "Okay, I can't be this, I can't have that. But look at what I do have. I've got this great heart. This great personality. People like me. And I have this man I love in my life."

In my life I've worried a lot about how to help solve other people's problems. When I deal with a person who's really difficult, I think that's their illness. I try to determine where does that behavior come from. I'm going to get

to their wellness. I'm going to find a way into the good part, make them laugh, make them feel comfortable. And so when you flip that around, you make life so much easier for them and for yourself.

I tell young people there are three things you need to know. One is to learn forgiveness. The major spiritual doctrines begin with forgiveness: Man shall not judge, only I. The second thing: Time is not on your side. If you think it's on your side,

you're going to wake up and be forty and know that your dream did not happen. And the third thing: Nothing comes from nothing. You might want it. You might tell your friends about it. You may dream it, but you need to make it happen. Opportunity may knock, but you have to be actively seeking it. And whether you make it happen depends on how you respond. ■

Ari DeSano

I'm Ari DeSano. I work at the Los Angeles LGBT Center in the marketing department. For my own enjoyment I also perform and write songs—I describe them as humorous social commentary. I've created a character named Odious Ari. He's a 103-year-old vaudevillian, and he has a lot of things to say about the world.

I grew up in Ohio, in the suburbs outside of Cleveland during the seventies and eighties. It's a pretty conservative part of the country. My parents became born-again Christians. Growing up then in that region, while coming to terms with my sexuality and my gender identity, was very difficult. I was worried that I would lose my family and my friends. It affected my self-confidence and my feelings of worth. I'm still working on it.

I'm nonbinary. That's a rejection of the binary system that categorizes things as one or the other—A or B, black or white, straight or gay, male or female. Nonbinary can be both or neither. And I think of it as neither, because I don't feel completely male and I don't feel completely female. I reject the notion that there are only two categories. I've heard people say *gender fluid,* and I like that term too because it suggests that you're moving in between two things.

My view of what makes a person valuable, lovable and worthwhile has changed over time. People around me influenced my thinking then. I have come to understand the world in a different way. Now I think for myself. If I don't judge other people, and I don't judge myself, I can value and appreciate people more and appreciate myself more.

My parents did accept my sexuality. I was able to bring home partners. I was worried about their rejection and that didn't happen. In fact, they were very welcoming. Young people should be careful, though. There are those times when a kid is feeling like I can do this, I'm empowered, I'm going to do it. And they come out and their parents aren't accepting. You have to work within the world that you are in at that moment.

If I could go back and advise my younger self—or someone in a similar position today— I'd say there's nothing wrong with you. People around you might be saying something's wrong and you need to fix it. But remember that who you are is not something to be fixed. The more I have embraced who I am and explored that, the happier I've been.

During those times when you may have doubts about your self-worth, imagine yourself in thirty years looking back and thinking, "I love that kid. That kid's great." ∎

Who you are is not something
to be fixed. The more I have…

...embraced who I am and explored that, the happier I've been.

Craig Thompson

I'm Craig Thompson. I'm the chief executive of APLA Health, the successor organization to the AIDS Project, Los Angeles. We provide health care to low-income LGBT folks across Los Angeles County and people living with HIV and AIDS.

I grew up in eastern Washington state—where the apples come from. My father was a dentist, and my mother was a nurse and then a homemaker. That was a very "fiftyish" time. So what to me and my sisters seemed boring, to my parents was safe and secure. My parents weren't narrow-minded. They were educated and well read. They just hadn't been exposed to gay people.

I knew at about age eight to ten that I was gay. By the time I got into junior high I started to have sexual thoughts. There was no literature out there, no stories out there about gay people. But I pretty quickly figured out that there were men I was attracted to, and I could have sex with men.

"I moved to New York to redefine myself as the someone who I knew I always was."

I came out very late, after law school. I was very timid. So I kept pushing myself to take more risks, moving to places, doing things. I moved to New York from Seattle to redefine myself as someone who I knew I always was. I wasn't prepared for a lot of things that life throws your way. You suddenly get out in the world and people die and financial hardships come and not everybody's nice to you.

We were all working in corporations. We all wore suits every day. Nobody was out at work. And then on weekends during the summer we went to Fire Island. The first time I took the ferry across and looked around, I thought this is what Disneyland is supposed to be like: all gay men just being themselves for the entire weekend. And then on Sunday afternoon you got on the boat back to the city, got up the next morning and worked all week, until you could go back on Friday.

I worked with a pretty buttoned-down crowd that was focused on traditional goals of success. As a gay person in my firm, you may not be promoted as quickly as others. You needed a wife or a girlfriend to go to dinner parties with you. And if you came by yourself, it wasn't as easy to mingle with the partners and their wives as it was for the younger executives who came with girlfriends or wives. When it came to promotion, the intangibles can work against you. Do partners think you're a good guy—somebody they'd like to hang out with?

When I found out I was HIV positive, it wasn't even called AIDS—it was "this disease." The news accounts and most physicians referred to it as acquired—a lifestyle disease. So all the way up to the mid-1980s, the belief was that as long as you weren't extremely promiscuous, as long as you didn't do a lot of drugs, you were going to be okay. But then by about 1984 or 1985 you started to hear reports that you can get this disease just from one contact.

And I remember having this wonderful thirtieth birthday party on Fire Island. But it was also sad because I was pretty sure that I wasn't going to live to thirty-one. I had just lost two or three really close friends.

I wanted to go to business school but thought it doesn't make any sense to spend the last couple of years of my life in school. But I decided I'm not going to live my life as if I'm going to die but as if I'm going to live. So I went back to business school and loved it.

And when I graduated, my partner and I moved to Los Angeles. I got a job in a large bank working in its legal department, and he joined a law firm.

I had the opportunity eventually to go to work in a non-profit serving people with HIV. So I left the bank job thinking I'd rather spend whatever time I have left working in this community. I went from living with HIV, assuming I was going to die, to being someplace where people were dying. That was 1991. That's what I still do. It has been fascinating, interesting, and challenging work.

There was a movement recently to put an AIDS monument in West Hollywood. The organizers wanted me to get involved. I told them I understand this project will be truly cathartic and helpful for you guys—to go back and remember. For me it would be very painful.

I'd rather funnel all that pain into doing the work I'm doing now: supporting LGBTQ health, helping young gay men avoid this disease, and ending the epidemic. ∎

Madonna Cacciatore

I'm Madonna Cacciatore, and I'm the executive director of Christopher Street West/LA Pride. I'm also an actor, so I often say I have two lives.

Christopher Street West is a nearly fifty-year-old organization that produces the LA Pride Festival. Working with our board, we are also exploring creating an entire development program for LGBTQ people that could include arts, education, and scholarships. That means I'm in the community a lot working with LGBTQ and straight allies in the cause.

My family is from New York, but we ended up in a small town in Texas because my dad was in the military. We eventually moved to Irving, near Dallas, and lived there for many years.

My greatest challenge in my life was my brother's death. He died from AIDS during the early years of the epidemic when we were just figuring out what it was.

The epidemic became very personal for me when my brother got sick. I spent a lot of time in New York with him and his partner. I became an activist. I was working with people with AIDS. They were sick and in hospitals. People were wasting away and dying. I tried to be with them, holding their hands, letting them know they're loved.

While this time presented my greatest challenge, it was also the most beautiful thing in my life. People came together in a way that they don't do unless there's something this horrific happening. We felt our community really pull together in a way that was unprecedented. It was a time that changed my life.

Love was the only response possible. There was nothing else that could help. The focus was very clear. Love was ever present. It was like we were almost on autopilot because we had to just keep moving forward. We were constantly losing people, going to memorials. Seeing these beautiful men, who were suffering so much, discriminated against, and even hated by some communities and by some religions, was very hard for me. But at the time we didn't even think; we were just doing, doing, doing.

I got involved in working with charities and events that raised money to help fight AIDS, including my volunteer time at "The Quilt" for the NAMES Project. I eventually went to work for the AIDS Project Los Angeles. The work changed my focus. It helped me see that I could not be totally caught up in so much of the drama in the world because there were so many forces that attacked

We get to create this world today.
Art, creativity and connection are fuel for our souls. Read a script, create a character, draw something, sing, dance, go to the theater, ride a bicycle on a quiet road, help a stranger.
Fuel your soul.

us all the time. My work today helps me keep my focus on the love and energy in the world, and I surround myself with people who want to create positive change. The work I do has helped me stay true to my soul and become who I am.

I decided to come out when I was very young. I tried to date boys and it wasn't horrible, but I wasn't having a great time. I had a big crush on my French teacher in high school and knew it. I just thought she was so pretty and I wanted to hang around her all the time. I thought, "That can't be normal." But it didn't feel weird to me. And then later I kissed a woman when I was probably twenty years old. But when I kissed that woman the first time I was like, "Oh wow, that's what it is. This is it." And then I knew who I was.

I came out to my parents pretty quickly. My mom loved everybody. She said that she just wanted me to be happy, and she loved me no matter what.

My dad did the whole Italian thing: "You need to find a guy and just have sex so you can be straight." And I was like, "No, I'm not doing that." And then in the Italian fashion he threw all my clothes on the bed: "You can just ..." But then he softened and said, "All right, well, maybe we should just invite her over. What do you want for dinner?"

And I was confused but thought, "Okay." It turned out to be the most awkward dinner you could imagine. But he never judged me. He loved me no matter what.

I read a blogger recently who comes from a Christian tradition but who speaks from the correct side of things, in my opinion. His name is John Pavlovitz, and he wrote something like, "Blessed are the damn-givers for they will right side the world." And that moved me.

Another mentor I've learned so much from is the actress Dee Wallace who led a master acting class I was in for three years with a group of amazing people. She used to say: "What are you focused on? That's your life." And so I always think about where I'm putting my energy. And when I'm really pissed off about a lot of things that are happening, I am reminded to stay focused because that's where I'm going to head. If I'm focused on all these negative things, without realizing it I will end up going in that direction.

So you can't turn left and right at the same time. You have to make a decision. What are you focused on? Well, that's your life. ■

Buck Angel

My name is Buck Angel. I was born female but had a sex change to become a male twenty-two years ago. I'm fifty-six years old, so I did this in my late twenties when nobody else was doing it in Los Angeles. Bottom surgery was not possible for me then, so I don't have a penis. I have a vagina.

My vagina is very famous. I was the first transsexual man to create the platform of trans male pornography. I was known as the man with the pussy. Mark Quinn is a well-known British sculptor who created a full nude sculpture of me that was purchased by the Museum of Art in Adelaide, Australia. My body has become my platform and the driving force behind my activism. I'm a man with a vagina, and I wasn't going to let that fact stop me from living in the world as a man.

It's easy to be a victim. It's not easy to be a survivor, but it will change your life. You'll look at it like a gift, and when you have gratitude in your life, everything is different.

I've become a human rights activist who believes in creating a space for everybody. We don't need to conform to our society's ideas. We need to conform to our own ideas. I started to have people question what is masculinity and femininity. What is a man and what is a woman?

I grew up in the sixties and the seventies in the San Fernando Valley. I was a tomboy, which my parents accepted because they always thought I was going to grow out of it. But I didn't grow out of it. I like to say I grew into it. But, believe me, from the age of about fifteen when I started puberty until I was twenty-eight, my life was horrifying. I started to grow boobs and I got my period and nobody knew what to do with me. I became a very angry person.

I was an athlete. That was the place that was very masculine for me. I became a sought-after runner. I was excelling in my running, but drugs and alcohol became part of my life because I was a very sad person. I became what they call a cutter. I used to take razor blades and cut my arms and cut my face and cut my breasts and cut everything. And I ended up in a psychiatric hospital.

My poor mom and dad were lost. They tried to take me to psychiatrists and therapists. They just kept telling me I was a gay woman. They would equate my sexuality with my gender.

Because I was a masculine woman, they immediately said, "Well, you're really just a lesbian." And I'm like, "Actually, no, I'm really a man."

I became a fashion model as a woman. I was taken to Europe. But alcohol and drugs were my life, and I didn't last very long in Europe because I just was not showing up. I ended up back in Los Angeles, homeless. My family disowned me. I had nothing.

I learned how to create a place for myself by prostituting as a little boy. I would dress up with a baseball cap and baggy pants and strap my boobs down with an ace bandage. Old men would pick me up on Santa Monica Boulevard. And when you're a drug addict and an alcoholic, you're very smart and you figure out ways to make money to buy cocaine.

I really think my will to live saved me from that awful place. It was like I was enlightened for one second by whoever said to me "This is your life." I got sober and I've been sober for thirty years. I did whatever I needed to do to get off of the streets.

And with my sobriety I figured out that I would have the sex change. But I discovered there were no doctors for women who wanted to become men. There were only doctors for men becoming women in Los Angeles. One doctor I spoke with told me, "I have never worked with a woman who wants to become a man. I've done this for over thirty years and I've done it for men becoming women. But I'm willing to try this with you, but you're basically going to be my guinea pig." I had no choice. It was life or death for me.

Today I celebrate life so much. It should have been taken away from me, but it wasn't. Now I get to give back to a community that gave to me. I get to help save lives. I get to educate the world about what it means to be a person. I get to wake up every day and show up. I get people to listen—to celebrate life. I've been given a second chance and I know that. Because I chose to walk the survivor's path, I'm here today. ∎

CONNECTED

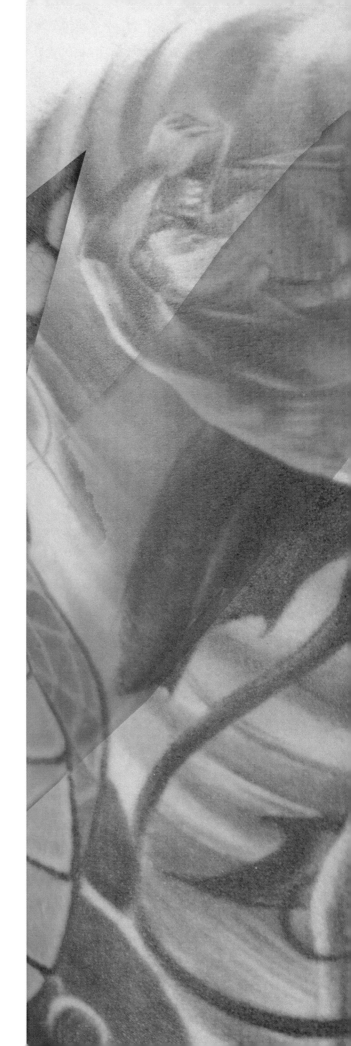

Andrew Ableson

My name is Andrew Ableson and I'm an actor. I studied creative arts at university in Nottingham, England. I discovered I preferred the performing arts, especially multimedia work that was collectively devised and site-specific. It was extremely creative as the work often did not depend on a conventional script. After college I had my own theatre company, which eventually led to more mainstream acting. I've been doing that ever since, on stage, screen, voice-over, commercials, and cabarets.

I grew up on the borders of London, the green belt, where city turns into country. My father was the well-known crooner Frankie Vaughan—England's Sinatra or Tony Bennett. When I was off school, I'd go on tour with him and watch him from the wings. I saw how fulfilled he was creatively and was drawn to performing, whether I knew it then or not.

This business demands you have nerves of steel to handle rejection. You tell yourself when you get passed over for a part that they wanted someone with a different look, and it *isn't* about you. But it *is* about you. I try to develop a sense of calmness and strength to keep doing it and not take the rejection down into my soul.

Still, every time I'm about to step on stage, I'm terrified. I love it once I'm on, but I still get jittery because I know I have to meet the expectations of every person in that audience. I have to put any fear out of my mind and connect with them honestly. A self-aware performance always grates.

Having people around me who love me provides me with the backbone I need to deal with rejection and fear.

I make sure I have love, as much as I can, in all my relationships: with my family, with my husband, with my friends. I value honesty over everything. I strive for absolute honesty and truth.

My parents had always told me, "As long as you're happy, we're happy." I knew this was a veiled recognition of my sexuality. I had friends who had come out to their family almost as a spiteful act. They told them midway through a fight, "Oh, and by the way, I'm gay." Then their relationship with their parents would suffer for a while after. It saddened me. Coming out as gay was not that problematic personally, although I didn't "officially" tell my mom until I was around thirty. Ridiculous. My father had already passed away. I had, however, told my grandmother years before.

Truth and love can carry you through anything.

She was the one who took care of me a lot when my parents would go on tour. She asked Dominic, my partner, "Do you love my Andrew?" He (luckily) said, "Yes."

"Well, I love you then," she said. She was wonderful.

Whenever I can practice calmness, patience, and gather as much love around me as possible, I feel I can deal with just about any challenge. Two years ago I had open-heart surgery. I dealt well with it because I thought that I'd already had a wonderful life, and if I didn't come out of the operation, so be it. I wasn't going to achieve anything by freaking out. There's already enough in the world to freak out about. I think I may be a closet hippie. ■

Everything else is far less important.

You've got to
be strong and
have a spine
of steel and
be willing
to stand up
for what
you believe.

My name is Robert Clement. I am ninety-three years old and a bishop of the American Catholic Church. Even though I retired decades ago, there's no such thing. So I'm still active in my church.

I grew up in Wilkes-Barre in northeastern Pennsylvania on the edge of the Pocono Mountains. It was originally a coal-mining town and a melting pot for European immigrants in the early twentieth century. The male side of my family had emigrated from Poland. The other side was Anglo-Saxon. My upbringing was ordinary; you might even say very plain. I had an older brother who died about a year ago. I have a sister who is eighty-six or eighty-seven and still lives in that area.

Our small town was not too far from New York City, so as a young man I took the bus most every weekend to the city. New York City was the center of the universe back then. It represented a totally different life—a different way of living.

As a young priest I had led a quiet life, serving straight parishes in New Jersey. But when Stonewall exploded in 1969, I had left that behind and was living a very gay life with a man in the West Village. On the night it happened, I was walking up West Fourth. My companion said, "There's something going on over there." He got a closer look and reported, "There's a lot of gay men, and they're doing high kicks at the police." We weren't going over there to find out why people were doing high kicks at the police. So we continued home while Stonewall was happening. In a sense we missed it.

Within a day or two the feeling within the LGBT community changed tremendously. We came together as a group. When I learned the details of what happened at Stonewall, I said something that Martin Luther King said at another time: "I'm free, I'm free, I'm free, and I'm never going back." On the one-year anniversary of Stonewall in 1970, I leapt out of the closet. I was at the first liberation march on Fifth Avenue. The Time magazine coverage of the event included a photo of me with my lover dressed in full religious garb. We were kissing and carrying a sign showing the Holy Ghost descending upon the assembled. It read, "Gays, this is your church."

I always supported the concept that God's love is universal—that God's love is also for LGBT people. I wanted to stand out as a symbol that religion is for everyone and God is with everyone. I began to concern myself with starting an independent parish for LGBT people.

There were two things I had to overcome. The first was the Church itself. When I came out, I had been very active with what was called the Polish National Catholic Church. They were archly conservative and they had fits when I came out, even going so far as to deny that I had ever been a priest in their jurisdiction. I fought it. I told them this is what I see as my work and God's work, and it's what I'm going to do. So they sent a monsignor to find out what I really was about. I placed my ordination certificate under heavy shatterproof glass just in case anything crazy were to happen. And standing right with me when he arrived was a very good friend with a leather boyfriend.

They backed off. There was nothing they could do. And so I began my new church work based on the idea that God is for everyone including gay people. And back then there were no sympathetic parishes.

We were a pariah. We were on the edge of society at best.

We handed out leaflets at the first liberation march announcing our first Mass would be Sunday afternoon two weeks later. We had no idea what to expect at the Episcopal church we had rented. About fifteen minutes before Mass was scheduled to begin, we didn't see anyone. So we thought there would be few in attendance. At 2:00 pm we opened the doors and a crowd packed the church and filled the aisles. It was standing room only—maybe five hundred or more people. It was a big thing.

One of the first observances we presided over was a Holy Union ceremony—what we call today Holy Matrimony—between two people. I realized that the male partner was actually still physically a woman, but that didn't deter me. That ceremony joined a person we now call a transgender-male with a female partner. At that time the person would have been referred to as a transvestite.

Another important challenge I had to overcome in my life my gaining my family's acceptance of my new life and mission. When I came home to tell my mother about my work, she told me that she didn't want any of those people in our lives. It took about two years for my mother to realize I wasn't going to change. I wasn't going to go back to some standard religious thing. Later on, one of my nephews, who had a good position with Procter and Gamble, led the fight at P & G to support the gay movement. He was a very positive out young man. And that softened the blow.

I'm always a little surprised about the attention I receive. I don't do things in the hopes of attracting people around me. I do them because I feel they have to be done. If the rest of the world is in a heterosexual closet, there's no room for us. ■

Darren Stein

My grandparents started a boutique film lab in Hollywood in the sixties. My dad would come home from work and scrub his hands to get off the chemicals. Film was always in my blood. The kids on my cul-de-sac in Encino were younger than me, so it was easy to convince them to act in my films. I had a currency on that close-knit street that I didn't have at the sports-oriented all-boys school I went to from age twelve to seventeen. I ended up going to film school at NYU and made my first feature five years later.

Don't be afraid
to embrace
what you think
might be the
strangest
aspects of
yourself.
You'll be
surprised
how many
people
will find
strength
in you.

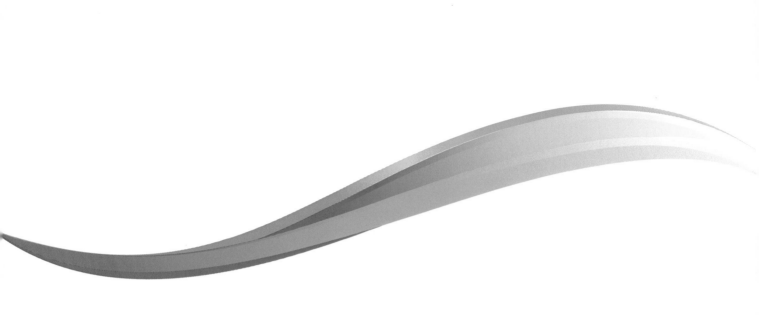

I always knew I was different from the other kids, very much an outsider with bizarre sensibilities. My queerness has been a part of my identity from as early as I can remember. At seven or eight, I was drawn to the collision of horror and glamour in films like *The Hunger* and *The Rocky Horror Picture Show*. I've always had an attraction to the forbidden, the fringier aspects of the world, the underbelly of society.

When I went to college, one of my parents' dearest friends, who was like an uncle to me, died of AIDS. When I came out to them as a sophomore, my mom was terrified this would happen to me. It was easier for her not to talk to me than to deal with it, so we became estranged for a year. My dad was more accepting, having gone through his nephew's coming out several years earlier. He told my mom she had to accept me, and they nearly got divorced over it. Not long after coming out, I fell in love with a guy, and we ended up being together for eight years. He and my mom became incredibly close, and she regretted the year they didn't meet.

There's no question that accepting my sexuality helped me to be a more authentic filmmaker. The vast majority of directors are white, cisgender heterosexual males. I'm grateful for my queer, outsider perspective. ■

Greg "G Spot" Siebel

I'm Greg Siebel, but everybody calls me G Spot. I'm an assistant designer at a dress company that makes dresses for little girls and juniors.

I grew up in Schenectady in Upstate New York. I was mostly left to my own devices as a kid. My dad was an alcoholic so he wasn't very present in my life. I was mature for my age and my mom left me alone a lot. When my dad left, the protection I felt from having this man in the household was gone. I was always a sensitive kid. I wasn't into sports and I was an easy target. I was horribly bullied. And then my friend's older brother molested me. I never knew the language or had the ability to tell anybody this was happening. So I just swallowed all those emotions, which made it really easy to become addicted to drugs and alcohol.

There's a way to come out of the darkness and …

I started really young. When I was nine I stole two bottles of wine and my friends and I drank it. I don't know what everybody else was thinking, but all I could think was, "I can't wait to do this again." And so that led me down a path of destruction that lasted many years.

After I moved to New York City I had a wild style. I would wear big hair and tons of makeup. I was a kind of androgynous David Bowie glam. I met this woman in the Village who started promoting parties at the Pyramid Club. I became her assistant, the go-go dancer, and the cohost. She was looking at me one night and said, "I can't call you Greg when you're all dressed up like this; it's just not flashy enough. You need a fun, glamorous club name. Gigi? No, that sounds too girly." My initials are GS. And then she finally says, "I'm gonna call you G Spot." And from the moment she uttered it, no one ever knew that I had another name.

I worked in clubs until five, six in the morning, and everybody around me was drinking and partying, and no one was telling me that it was out of control. I knew at my core that I wasn't sure where I was supposed to be, who I was supposed to be, or what I was supposed to be doing with my life. But I knew that I was the only person who was stopping me from getting there. I felt so bankrupt inside. I just didn't want that anymore. Facing those demons and getting sober was the hardest challenge of my life.

Now I pursue a spiritual life in my recovery and I take it very seriously. It's not easy.

There's a way to come out of the darkness and into the light, if you really just believe in yourself. When I was younger, I was ashamed that I was different—and those feelings were a hindrance. I like to be glittery and flashy—show myself as a very colorful character. That's what makes me, me. It's the opposite of a hindrance. I feel like that's just a reflection of how I feel on the inside. I try to exude positivity and happiness. You know, it's almost impossible for a little kid to think like that. You may not feel any happiness or joy. But eventually if you find your tribe things do get better. ■

...into the light, if you really just believe in yourself.

Life is embarrassing if lived properly.

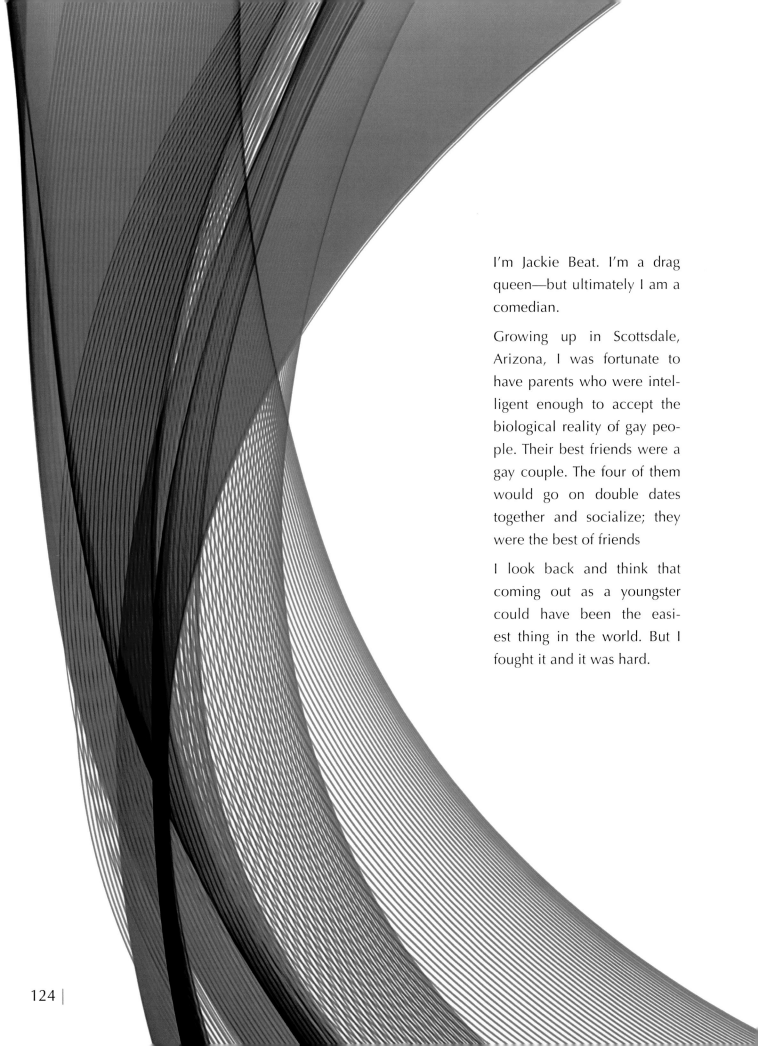

I'm Jackie Beat. I'm a drag queen—but ultimately I am a comedian.

Growing up in Scottsdale, Arizona, I was fortunate to have parents who were intelligent enough to accept the biological reality of gay people. Their best friends were a gay couple. The four of them would go on double dates together and socialize; they were the best of friends

I look back and think that coming out as a youngster could have been the easiest thing in the world. But I fought it and it was hard.

I felt everyone was just *assuming* I was gay because I knew every line to *The Carol Burnett Show*. I knew I could sing, but I sounded like a girl. And I thought that was humiliating then. The irony is now I make my living singing as a woman.

There were other challenges. I was a fat kid. And I was gay. Sports—any sport—became a nightmare. I was always the last one chosen. It was humiliating. But I didn't blame them: I wouldn't pick me either. I didn't want to be picked at all. I wanted to go to the library.

I could be very polarizing in school: people either loved me or hated me. I was funny, and I used my humor in my defense. If you were bullied or you knew there was a threat of being beaten up, you became funny fast. If you could make somebody laugh and get them on your side, they were like, "Oh, maybe I won't punch you. You made me laugh."

Even in school, I knew I didn't want to be *them*. I thought they seemed really boring. They're going to grow up and get married and have kids— which is fine for them. I think I'd rather be me.

But 99 percent of what I saw of the world during the '60s and '70s was through movies, rock stars, music, and television— and all of it was heterosexual. So I asked myself, "How will I fit into this future?"

And my answer was *as a creative performer*. I watched *The Rocky Horror Picture Show* midnight on Saturdays and saw people like me who were crazy and weird. Not only did they see nothing wrong with it, they were celebrating it.

I literally came out of the closet and became a sexually active gay man the day AIDS gave its first press conference. I was finally free to be who I was, and there's this horrible thing that was tainting everything and taking people away— amazing creative people.

I was very careful and, I must admit, fearful.

We're human. People were drinking and some were doing drugs. Some never got enough love and affection as a child or denied that they were gay. In those days you couldn't go to the prom with a guy. You didn't have kids. You didn't have the usual pressure to provide for a growing family. You're like, "This whole life is about me and having a good time." So when they finally came out they went a little crazy, trying to make up for lost time. Things are a lot better now. A lot of my friends have adopted kids. There are a lot of choices now. I like that.

Here's a favorite quote of mine that helps me get through the rough patches: Life is embarrassing if lived properly. And I believe it. So many people go through life always careful not to embarrass themselves. It's like they live their lives on the red carpet and never take a chance. Nobody wears the swan dress like Björk. Nobody dresses up like Cher with feathers and goes a little crazy. Maybe twenty years from now you will go, "My God, what was I thinking?"

But I'd rather say "What was I thinking?" than "That was a nice boring outfit." If you live your life properly, there should be photographs of you with a terrible hairstyle that was in fashion at the time and you thought looked great.

And now you're like, "Oh boy, what was I thinking?" ■

Rain Valdez

My name is Rain Valdez. I am an actress. I also write, direct, and produce films. I am founder of an artist collective called Now More Than Ever, where creative LGBTQ people work together to produce the content they create. Since our inception, we've completed a web series and two short films.

I was born in the Philippines, but I grew up in Guam. My biological father died before I was born. When my mom married my stepdad, he was living in Guam so we moved there when I was about four. There were five of us kids: I had an older sister from my biological father, and my stepfather had three children.

The biggest challenge I faced growing up was overcoming everyone else's idea of who I should be. I was assigned "male" at birth; but it wasn't that simple. I was told that I was born intersex: I was both female and male. A third gender in a way. There wasn't really a word for that in Guam. In the Native American culture

Every day I get up,
gather my drive,
my vision and
my determination
and search and search
for a place of belonging,
and when I don't find it,
I create my own space.
Lather, rinse and repeat.

the term for these special people is *two spirits,* and they are revered for the spiritual connections they bring into the world. But in Guam and the Philippines, we didn't have a similar concept because once those countries were colonized the binary mentality was infused into our culture and society.

I knew at a very young age that I was a girl and wanted to grow up to be a strong, kick-ass, and hardworking woman. But everyone else had different ideas. So I had to find ways to stick to what I believed in and battle through all the challenges others put in my way. I was lucky enough to have a mother who believed in me. She knew that I was different but found her way to love me.

I went to a Catholic school in Guam; the country and the schooling were very traditional. People didn't believe that trans people had a place in the world. If you were trans the consensus was that you're going to hell. It was a challenge for me to not believe that and not live within everyone else's truths. I needed to have my own truth and live within my truth. As I moved around in the world, I was constantly being "otherized" or told that I didn't fit. It was hard to wake up every day and do it all over again. I had to fight, really, for my own existence.

My strength came from within. I dug deep and became introspective. Once there, I was able to feel or see certain things about myself. The challenge was finding the courage to love whatever it was inside of me that was different from everyone else's perception of who I was. So when I chose to love it and nurture it and take care of that inner essence, I started to not really care about anyone else's opinions of me.

There were times when I was more androgynous or more gender queer, but I always leaned into being very feminine. The more I leaned into it, the more comfortable I felt, and the more other people were uncomfortable. Those who weren't afraid of knowing who I was saw confidence and courage. They saw someone who knew who she was. And those were the people that I surrounded myself with.

Another challenge I face is finding a loving relationship. But from men's perspectives there is still a lot of stigma, a lot of shame, associated with a man-trans woman relationship. I know it can exist for me, but I may not find it or even need it in my life today. I may just be enough in this world; my purpose may be to continue being a part of this movement with my sisters and the community. ■

COMMUNITY

Brigit Biagiotti

Rise above those who fall below.

My name is Brigit Biagiotti. I manage a program that assists in the effort to reduce the juvenile offender recidivism rate. The program keeps our youth in their home communities by providing meaningful community-based interventions.

I grew up outside of Philadelphia with my parents and three older sisters.

My first great challenge in life came early but lingers in my memory.

When I was twelve, I had to deal with my grandmother's sudden death. I actually went into my bedroom, refusing to come out for multiple days. At that time Mom told me, "The world's going to keep going on no matter if you're in it or not." This made me realize, "Alright, I'm just going to be in here and deal with it." I finally realized that no one was going to make me feel better about not having my grandmother anymore in my life. I just had to get up and just start going through the motions. Life became more manageable each day.

I've also had to deal with serious back injuries. I had initially injured my back playing ice hockey and then reinjured it in a slip-and-fall accident. I damaged my spine so badly that I had two surgeries, one leading up to a spinal fusion. I was out of work for over a year while trying to get on with my life. I was devastated. I had lost my athletic body to this injury, a big part of who I was.

To cope I kept busy—cooking a lot, walking. At first I couldn't walk well. Then I would slowly increase my distance. I was reminded how I dealt with my grandmother's death: I had to keep moving. No matter what, I had to keep moving. I think if you keep your body and brain in motion, your heart will naturally catch up. That helped me through my decision to come out to my family during my college years. I was enrolled at a Catholic university, and I was hesitant to share my secret with my family for fear of rejection.

After a major breakup with my significant other, I decided I would come out to my sister first. I could talk to her about anything. She never judged me; she always made me feel safe. She told me that she and others already had their suspicions. With that, I drove to my mom's house to tell her right away.

I walked into my mom's bedroom and said, "Mom, I have something to tell you." I mentioned my girlfriend's name and said something like she's not just a friend.

Her response: "Yes, she's your best friend."

And I was like, "No, she's my girlfriend, Mom. We've been together."

She had been painting in the bedroom. I remember the paintbrush was still in her hand. She stopped midstroke and just sat down on the bed with a blank stare. Her face spoke loudly; my mom never suspected anything.

My sister pushed me in the way that I needed to be.

Remembering how I had coped with my physical challenges, I knew we as a family had to keep moving. Both my parents and the entire family wanted to learn and understand where I was coming from. They needed to know that I'd be okay in a world that wasn't too accepting at the time.

Years ago my mom shared something that has stayed with me since. She told me, "Always rise above those who fall below." For me, that means that no matter what someone's opinion of you is, strive to rise above. Don't let anyone stand in your way of accomplishing your dreams and sharing your love with whoever that person may be, regardless of gender.

I try to live out this mantra each day in facing the obstacles in my life. I hope, too, it will continue to strengthen me as I encounter the inevitable challenges that await me. ■

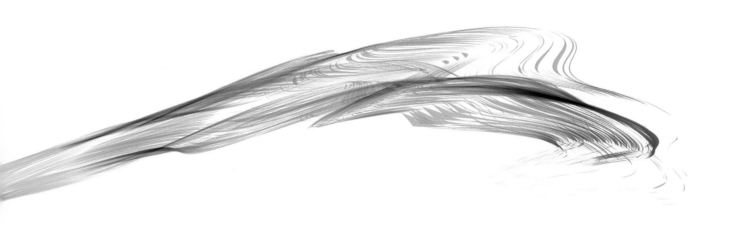

Kim Smith

*Dawn & Desiree —
Here's to better days!
Kim Smith*

I am Kimberly Denise Smith on paper, and Kim Smith to my friends. For the past twenty-three years, I've been a personal trainer and group fitness teacher.

I grew up in southern Kentucky, just north of the Tennessee border with my father and my stepmother. She ran a babysitting business out of our home. From the age of eight until eighteen, I was the worker bee around that house.

The biggest obstacle that I've had to overcome was being physically and verbally abused as a child. When my dad married my stepmother we all moved in with her, under her roof. Then the physical and verbal abuse began. I was only eight years old. She would throw things at me. She would hit me with things. She would spank me with belts, yardsticks, switches, whatever was handy. And then I would hear, "Your mother doesn't want you and you're fat and you're useless."

My father knew. I would have the marks. I would not be in school for a few days, or I couldn't do the chores around the house. But he did not have the capacity somehow to get us out. I should have talked to someone at our church or a teacher at school. I wasn't confident enough then. It's hard when you're in a situation like this, especially as a kid.

When I look back today, I know that I began to surmount this obstacle when my physical education teacher introduced us to the weight room. I was fifteen, and I discovered I had a good capacity for lifting. I was lifting more than most of the boys at fifteen. I was strong because we had big dogs, and I'd been lifting babies and kids for years. It never crossed my mind before that I could fight back. And when I did fight back—I broke my stepmother's nose when I hit her—that was definitely a turning point. She didn't physically bother me again.

In my late teens, I was busy with my first job, going to school, and trying to live with my stepmother without any physical interaction. But three days after my eighteenth birthday, I gathered my things and announced, "I'm out." I had been squirreling away clothes in preparation. As I walked toward the door that evening with my bag, my stepmother said to my dad, "Go get my gun."

And he did. It was a very small gun, and I'm very happy that she had poor aim because she shot at me that night. I didn't tell anyone about it. I was just happy to be gone. I didn't have any communication with them for several months.

Because that whole experience was so bad, I often wish I could have had a longer relationship with my birth mother. I missed out on many years with her. She died when I was thirty-three and I'm forty-two now. I lost lots of years with her. And I don't have a relationship with my father and I'm okay with that. It's something I've chosen.

I never thought I would have a stable relationship with anyone because what I saw made me think, "That's how this works? Fuck that. I'm not going to have that."

I was around eighteen or nineteen when I knew that I was gay. Something was going on before that, but you didn't really talk about it in the South. You heard how bad gay stuff was and all the names and jokes. I did have boyfriends and did things. But at nineteen I decided I wasn't going back to the hetero side of things or even to the bisexual.

I was in a relationship that I thought might go somewhere. And I agonized for weeks before I told my birth mom. When I did, she looked at me, and she said, "Honey, it's okay. I knew." I hadn't been eating and I was nervous. And she's like, "I don't care who you're with, just be happy and don't hurt anybody." And so I feel very blessed to have had that coming out situation. It could have been so much worse. And it just was who I was. Just like I have tattoos. I have thumbnails. I'm a gay girl. ■

When I meet
young people today
who may find themselves
in an abusive situation,
I tell them that
you can get out.
You can become stronger.
It will get better.
Find someone
you can trust
in your circle
and reach out.

Robin McWilliams

My name is Robin McWilliams. I manage actors and writers. I also produce documentaries, podcasts, and books. My philosophy's always been if you have the ability and capability to help, why would you not? When people come to me and say "Here's what I have," I'm like, "I'm totally game; let's make it happen."

I grew up in Long Beach, and when I graduated from high school, I came up here to LA. I started out as an actor, so it was either move to New York and be in the theater or move to LA. I chose LA because the weather's a lot nicer.

Mom had four kids. I'm the only one who is in the arts. I'm the only one who does hair and makeup. My sisters are "brainiacs." They have a numbers mentality, and I have an arts and colors mentality. And I have one brother who is a mechanic. Although we are a very eclectic family, Mom raised us as though we were all the same no matter what.

And she encouraged us to do whatever we needed to do.

We moved a lot and it was always about fitting in our new neighborhoods and schools. I went to a different school every year until junior high, and I think that's why I'm such a social butterfly now. I had to learn how to fit in, introduce myself, and ask, "How can I help?" And we didn't grow up with money in any way, shape or form. So I think that's why I'm always on a constant give back. I take the skills I learned in my childhood and put them to good use today—not being afraid, not being shy, and always wanting to help.

I was always looking out for the underdog even though our family would qualify as underdogs. We were living on Salvation Army food baskets at Christmas and food stamps. Mom was working several jobs to pay the rent. We learned that helping others helped us deal with our own challenges. And I believe

too that extending a helping hand can break down walls. It gets the conversation started, and it helps us look at things another way.

Coming out gay was really not that difficult. My mom raised us to believe we were all the same. You could cut someone and it always will come out red. The first time I said to her, "This is my girlfriend," she was like, "Okay." It was that easy. She was young herself and that influenced how she raised us.

When people come to me today for help, I want their dreams to come true. And my wife tells me that I'm always doing good for others but never looking out for myself. But I am reaching my goals because it makes me happy when I see someone succeed. I'm like, "Hold on, let me help you with that. Okay. You got it. Go, go, go." ■

If you have the ability to

help, why would you not?

You have an internal compass that will never steer you wrong. You're always going to go the right way.

My name is Margaret Cho, and I am a stand-up comedian. I'm also an actor, a producer, and a writer. I do a little bit of directing here and there, too, plus a little bit of music. I'm sort of a polymath—a many, random jobs kind of person. I've done well with my work and am proud of that.

I grew up in San Francisco in a very interesting family. They were Korean immigrants who decided, for some reason, to go into the gay bookstore business in San Francisco in the seventies. While growing up as part of a very structured, very religious Korean household, I was thrown into the very active, electric world of gay men in the seventies, which was incredibly political and tumultuous. This was around the time that Harvey Milk was finding his bearings as a politician, getting elected, and then eventually being assassinated.

It was really powerful to be able to grow up in the gay community in such an exciting time. Even though we were outsiders, my family felt part of that community. But then the AIDS epidemic started around the mid-1980s and gradually got worse and worse. The plague affected people who worked with us, the people we were connected to. We lost a lot of people to AIDS. The entire neighborhood where we had our business collapsed because there were so many deaths. I was in my teens then and was noticing the small changes at first and then a really rapid shift in the way the community looked and all of the death, all of the destruction, and all of the incredible suffering. It was something that was unthinkable, yet it was happening right there before our eyes. But the epidemic was really ignored by the government. At first it was not really reported on in the news. You didn't have a sense that people outside of our community knew what was happening. It wasn't until later that people began to acknowledge what is was—and that we needed help; we needed a place to deal with our grief.

All the different aspects of my growing up in that community really shaped my worldview. I was starting to do comedy then, performing a lot at political rallies and at gay bars, starting to develop my style. The community gave me permission to be whoever I was. I was around people who were gay, lesbian, trans. Because there were so many people identifying where they were at in terms of their sexuality and gender, that arena was very safe.

And the expression of sexuality at that time was very different. In the early nineties everybody was looking to find a way to be sexual without being fluid bonded. There was an emphasis on safe sex and using condoms but also sex without touching—and exploring who you were. There was an emphasis, too, on being as outrageous as you wanted to be, and I found all of that so fun and so great. There's a lot of fashion involved with that and a lot of parading around in latex and leather. It's so San Francisco. So I emerged from a time when any sort of expression of your sexuality was welcomed.

Getting my career going presented its own challenges.

And the biggest was invisibility. There were no Asian-American voices or faces working in show business when I was starting in the late eighties, early nineties. And so feeling very invisible and trying to break through and create visibility where there was none was a huge, huge undertaking. Over time I've been able to chip away at it and just rely on being a stand-up comedian because as a comedian you don't need a network to give you a show. You don't need anybody to tell you that it's okay for you to do what you do—you just do it. Through my comedy I was able to survive all of that.

And now I think the barriers are broken: today there are greater numbers of Asian-American faces and voices out there. To have been the first was a great trial, but looking back, I know this was the right thing to do. Actually, it's good to just be yourself and to find real success there. It's a long road, but the journey has been really remarkable.

What I understand about life is that it's incredibly short and it's incredibly precious. It's vital to do all the things that you want; to really listen to your heart. Just don't doubt yourself. I think that we always want to doubt ourselves, but really it's so smart to just believe in yourself. ■

Dawn McCrory

I'm Dawn McCrory. I own a physical therapy practice in Culver City, California. We specialize in treating movement disorders with physical therapy, Pilates instruction, and personal training.

I grew up around the mid-Atlantic area—Virginia, West Virginia, and Pennsylvania. We moved around quite a bit while my dad was earning advanced degrees at universities in the area. Because of the work he did in graduate school, Dad was recruited by the CIA. He was with the CIA until he retired.

I knew as a very young person that I was different from everyone around me. In junior high, my friends were talking about how cute the boys were. I couldn't join in those conversations. My feelings were actually for my girlfriends. When I was seventeen, I had my first relationship with a girl. When it ended I was eighteen. She was seventeen. And her mom threatened me with statutory rape if I ever tried to contact her again.

When I was in my early twenties, I started seeing another woman. I moved to Oklahoma for this person while she was finishing up her last year of college. It didn't end well. I had had three years of college and I just trashed them all. I was just so confused and distraught. I didn't really know who I was or what I wanted to be. I didn't have a connection anywhere. My parents did not know because I did not feel safe telling them. I was afraid I was going to lose them even though I didn't really feel a part of them. When I was twenty-three, my mom actually came to me and said, "You know, if I didn't know any better, I would think you were gay."

And I said, "Well, I am."

And that was the beginning of the end. My family disowned me. My father told me to move out. I felt so alone. I think that's when I figured out that I had no one to rely on but myself. I needed to deal with life, buck up, and get it done. Whatever I was going to do, I was going to be the best at it. I wanted to be able to flip the situation around and show my family I am worth something.

I got odd jobs and then started doing tree pruning. But I woke up one morning and reasoned that I don't think I can be forty and do labor-intensive work. And that very day I got my butt back to college. By then I knew what I wanted to do. And I became a physical therapist.

I was pushing myself so hard in school to be the best while working full-time. My rela-tionship with my family was still unresolved. I had written my dad a letter that I had carried around for a long time and never mailed. But one day I just put it in the mail.

Two weeks later I got a call from my mom inviting me to dinner. It was the most awkward dinner because my letter was never mentioned. The disowning was never addressed. So I didn't push it. I'm fifty-nine and we've still never discussed that letter.

My parents love my wife, Kim, to pieces. When I go home and visit without her, they're like, "Why didn't she come? Where is she? What's going on?" When we invited them to our wedding in 2008, however, they did not come. Basically my mom was like, "You know, we love Kim, but we just don't feel you should be able to get married." And so that told me my parents don't really fully accept me. I love them to pieces, but I always have a little shield around me when I visit.

I've pushed myself to be the best of this and the best of that for many years. But that wanting to be perfect drove me into a horrible, stressful, and anxious place. Only recently have I realized that I don't have to be perfect, that I'm a good person, and that everything that I have in life I deserve. I don't have to push myself 200 percent to get it. I don't have to be more than who I am. ∎

I am enough.
I have nothing to prove,
nothing to hide, and
everything to gain
by living my truth.

LOVE

Dana Goldberg

I'm Dana Goldberg. I'm a professional comedian. I also host galas around the country and do live auctions for non-profits that need money, especially LBGTQ women's organizations that work with kids and support HIV/AIDS education. My job is to bring some laughter and levity to a very serious subject. I make people happy, and then I take all their money and give it to charity.

I grew up in Albuquerque, New Mexico. I was born into a traditional family that turned into a single-parent family in which two out of the three kids are gay. I'm gay. My older brother's gay, and my sister's straight. My brother and I kid her a lot. We tell her that as long as you act gay in public, we don't have a problem with it because you were born that way. It's not your fault.

My mother raised us alone, working three part-time jobs. There was little child support. And she did a hell of a job. We're all still alive and thriving, and she has turned into one of my best friends. I was eighteen when I came out of the closet. I was afraid that coming out might ruin the love that was there. After I told her I liked someone, she said, "What did you think I was

Don't subscribe to other people's dogma. You have one life. You have to live it. No one else is going to live it for you, and there is no one else like you on this planet.

going to do: look at her and go, 'You're a woman!' Look Dana, I love you. I have to go to work. I don't care who you sleep with. Just be careful." Then she left.

I think the biggest thing that I've had to overcome in my life—and it continues to this day—is that voice of self-doubt in my head: "You're not good enough. You're never gonna make it. Who wants to listen to your story? Why do you deserve to have fame?"

My challenge every day is to overcome those doubts and live my truth as an openly lesbian woman. I've learned to find my voice and be authentically who I am. I know that I do have something to say and people are listening. People come up to me after a show to say thank you. I've even had fans confess, "I usually don't like stand-up comedy, but you make me laugh." I met a woman recently who told me she lost her partner to cancer four years ago and hadn't been to a social event since. After the show, we're sitting there crying together. I made her laugh. She was so grateful for that cathartic moment and to be able to open up.

For someone who creates her own work, I need to motivate myself every day so that I can be proud of the work I'm putting into this world. What's next? How do I not stay stagnant? How do I keep moving forward when I feel overwhelmed?

I don't think about ten years down the road. I enjoy the moment as it is. I have a girlfriend right now. I have joy and love in my life, and I'm incredibly grateful to spend my time with someone who supports me 100 percent in my career and values everything that I am, flaws and all. And that feels amazing.

I think right now, unfortunately, it's really difficult to find any joy in this current administration. There is so much shit coming at us from every angle. You see this other side of the world that is homophobic and transphobic and racist. You always knew that they were there. Somehow they've gotten a voice and now they feel like they have the freedom to spew their hate as loudly as they want.

So I—and all of us—must overpower that voice with love and empowerment. My job as a comedian is to offer some reprieve from the insanity—even if it's just for an hour during my show when people can forget about what's going on and just breathe.

Because if we don't do that, we may all go crazy. ∎

In order to shine
your brightest,
you have to be
in the world and
participate exactly
as you were created.

Marc Samuel

My name is Marc Anthony Samuel. I work in television and film and as a voiceover actor.

I grew up in two different places. I was born in Chicago. And I also lived in Portland, Oregon. I have two brothers and one sister, and I'm the oldest. Several people in my life have occupied the role of mother: my grandmother, my stepmothers, and my actual mother who passed. My father has always been a constant. He's been a huge influence on my life, not only as a human being, but even in his career choice. He had been a stage actor in Chicago and gave it up to raise a family. I wanted to continue doing his work in my own career, and I did.

My dad's parents were from Jamaica; my mom's were American. We weren't spoiled by any means; we were lower middle-class. If we wanted something, we had to work for it. And if we didn't, we just didn't have it.

The most difficult challenge I had to overcome was this personal perspective on being a gay black man in an environment that I mistakenly understood to be anti-me. We do have a history in the United States of racism and homophobia. We do. It's there. But it doesn't harm us until we buy into the perspective of racism or homophobia, and we allow it to it erode our own self-worth.

I stopped and listened to my loved ones. I discovered that there were people who had been positively influenced simply by my existence—as just me. I saw that I had achieved goals that were important to me. And I thought, "Wait, I count. I am valuable. I'm so much more than just a 'gay black person.' That's just a small part of my larger tapestry." I'm a human being who can contribute and bring value to this thing called *life*. Once I started viewing my world in that light and understanding how wonder-

ful I could be, I began to take greater charge of this clown car we call life. I bent the steel that was my reality into a life of service, a life of art, a life of friendship, of humor and of reflection. The whole act of being an artist is to reflect or synthesize within your art that which is around you.

No matter what you do in your life, some people will like you; others won't. Some people will understand you; others will not understand you. At the end of the day, though, if you have a strong base of people—your family, coworkers, friends—who absolutely love you as you are and cheer you on, nothing else matters. It's go, go, go.

We are exactly the way we're supposed to be. Straying from who you are—what you have been blessed with—is a greater problem than anything else. In order to shine your brightest, you have to be in the world and participate exactly as you were created. ∎

Soozin Lewis

No matter what happens today, the sun will still come up tomorrow.

My name is Soozin Lewis. I live just outside of Philadelphia and work for the National Guard as a civilian doing sustainability and energy management

I was born and raised in South Florida, the Fort Lauderdale-Miami area. I'm an only child, and I grew up in a pretty typical household with lots of pets. My parents split up when I was eight or so. It was an amicable parting and everything was fine. My parents remained friends; there was never any animosity that I saw.

My memories are that my dad was always the silly one—playful and goofy and funny. My mom was more serious and the disciplinarian—putting structure in place and checking off boxes for life.

I spent more time with my mom after the split because I lived primarily with her after Dad moved out. Everything was comfortable. I went to school and followed my routine. When I stayed with Dad, who lived nearby, I got to decorate my bedroom. I could pick my bedspread and make the room what I wanted. But I always felt like I was somewhere different, and I think he wasn't always sure what

to even do with me. But they both tried their best.

But when I was fourteen, things got tougher: my dad killed himself.

His death was certainly the greatest hardship in my life. He was HIV positive, in the early nineties. I was about twelve years old when I found out about his disease. I was a smart kid; I was tuned in and I knew that this was really bad.

My parents typically spoke to me like an adult if I asked questions. They didn't try to hide things, and if they did I usually found out anyway.

As a result, I had to learn to grow up really quickly. I had to try to absorb and understand difficult and complicated information about his health. I remember seeing many pill bottles in the bathroom. I would read the labels and open the containers to look inside. My parents tried to protect me but they didn't lie. I would listen to conversations and pick things up. So that was challenging.

And when he decided to kill himself, it was awful. It was terrible. But looking back, I wasn't that surprised. I had a dream a few months prior to his death; in the dream he did that exact thing. And when I woke up from the dream, it took me twenty minutes to realize it was only a dream. So when it actually happened, it was very surreal.

I don't know how I dealt with this. I guess I just grew up. I just learned some really huge life lessons at a very early age: You never know what's coming tomorrow; you never

know how long someone's going to be around; you learn that every day matters. Things are suddenly so clear. I suppose I could have found unhealthy ways to cope—experimenting with drugs or making other bad decisions. But I had a good head on my shoulders. I'm sure my mom had a lot to do with that. Both of my parents were very well educated, very successful people. I did not see failure as an option.

When I went off to college, I really got this laser-beam focus, and I've been relentless in my pursuit of success ever since. I like setting goals and achieving them. I'm always wanting to strive for something more. I don't know if that has something to do with attempting to compensate for my loss; it's just who I am. I've never tried to pinpoint what's behind it.

I think my mother knew before I did, or before I was ready to accept, that I was gay. She asked me about it during high school, out of concern. I recall being very uncomfortable about the question. And I also clearly recall her explaining that it was completely fine if I was gay but to understand that not everyone out there would be as accepting as she was. She did not want me to mistakenly believe the rest of the world felt the same as those I was raised around. It was a gentle warning of homophobia and bigotry in our society. So, while I was not ready to own up to it yet, she instilled some important knowledge about society in a nonjudgmental way, regardless of where I fell on the spectrum.

During my college years, I was visiting my grandmother, and she asked me, "Do you have a boyfriend." I answered, "No, but I have a girlfriend." My mom asked why I came out to my ninety-year-old grandmother and not to her. I said I didn't feel that I had to, and she took it as a testament to our relationship. So I never actually "came out" to Mom. I just brought someone home at some point and she got it. All told, I had it really easy on this one.

I've got a lot of inner strength. I don't know if it's genetic or if I learned perseverance through experience. Probably some of both, but I have it. When it's been sink or swim, I didn't have a choice. I just had to handle what came and keep moving forward, and that's what I did. ■

Sue Sherman

I hope to see you + get to know you better

Sue

My name is Sue Sherman. I teach mathematics and coach tennis at a private high school in Los Angeles. I've proudly done it for thirty-two years.

I grew up in New York on Long Island with my two hard-working parents—a lawyer and a teacher—and an older brother who lives about three miles from me today. My childhood was just so much fun, plain and simple. And even though I played four sports—volleyball, tennis, swimming, and basketball—I always found time to get into a little trouble. I was one of those kids who thought school was six days a week since Saturdays were always detention. So even though my mom would frequently make her way down the "walk of shame" to the assistant principal's office, and I'd hear all about it when we got home, I was totally all right with that.

When I think of the challenges I've faced in my life, I honestly feel they fall into two categories—physical and emotional. There's the physical challenge I faced in my youth and the emotional challenge I endured just recently, and both have become defining experiences.

Forty years ago, during my sophomore year in college, I suffered a skydiving accident. When I exited the plane, instead of arching my back, I brought my knees up to my chest and I went into a spin. When the parachute finally opened, I'd broken all the ribs on my right side, torn my knees, and severely damaged my lower extremities. I was going full speed when I hit the ground, and even though I knew I was going to live, I couldn't begin to imagine how different life would be from that day forward. What amounted to a minute or two of free fall would affect the next ten years of my life.

The doctors told my parents that if I walked again—and it was a big *if*—it would be with a significant permanent limp. My father lovingly replied, "That's not really an option, so we're going to do what it takes." My knee was almost destroyed. I'd suffered serious nerve damage in my back and cracked my skull, affecting my focus and depth perception. And after several initial surgeries, the pain lingered, unresolved. Walking or even just standing became a daily struggle.

After countless visits with varied specialists, we finally found one who'd recently flown to the United States after working with figure skaters in Europe who struggled with similar issues. Ultimately, the doctor figured out that I had acute compartment syndrome and recommended immediate surgery to prevent permanent, irreversible muscle damage. The very next day they operated on four of the compartments in my leg to relieve the pressure that was decreasing blood flow to my nerves and muscle cells. Were it not for that procedure, I wouldn't be walking today.

The entire process from accident to full recovery took just over ten years. As my thirties began, I was walking without any pain and playing tennis multiple times a week. Throughout those challenging months then years, my parents never allowed me to wallow in a pity party. They were direct, plain, and supportive. This was my new reality, and they'd simply tell me, "If you want something, then go get it. If it's meant to be, it's up to me."

They didn't let me feel sorry for myself—far from it. They empowered me. Their unique form of encouragement helped me realize that when things are wrong, you fix them. And if you can't, then you own it. While we aren't able to prevent everything that happens to us, we certainly are responsible for how we react. I've never gone skydiving again, but I've lived up to that advice ever since.

The other challenge was emotional, and much more recent. As a high school teacher and coach, I adored my school, loved the students and parents, and truly enjoyed working with some of the greatest colleagues. The school stood for the values and principles I was raised to believe and affirm. As with most jobs, change was expected and I

If you want something, then go get it. If it's meant to be, it's up to me.

openly accepted it. However, a few years back we welcomed a new head of school, and, unfortunately, he quickly fell short of the school's mission and purpose.

After several years of dealing with what I considered his poor work ethic and lack of integrity, I found myself at the center of a defining community controversy. The head of school had been changing grades—including my students' grades—so not only was I confused and personally upset, but I was also concerned with the ease with which he was able to do it. After researching the issue, I found that it's illegal to change grades in public schools but not explicitly illegal in private schools. Why that is so still confounds me.

Nonetheless, after discussing the issue with friends and family, I realized something had to be done. Or more precisely, I had to respond. I supported an effort to bring the matter to the school's board of trustees. And after seven months of closed meetings, internal investigations, and a public outcry, the head of school finally stepped down. While the topic was heated on both sides and the atmosphere on campus became tense, I believe the school is in a better place today and its honor and integrity are in the forefront again.

When I look back on these two challenges that have defined me—one physical, the other emotional—I now see them as a continuous life journey. And the strength and resolve I've shown and passed on to my colleagues, students, friends, and family began with the lessons I learned from my parents, especially my dad. My father and I had a special and close relationship. My biggest regret in life is that I had never "come out" to him. Struggling with my identity didn't allow me to tell him before his death. His opinion meant the world to me. I had to come to terms after his passing that as strong as I thought I was, I still wasn't strong enough to tell him who I was in love with. Fortunately my mother, who is still alive, and I have discussed my sexuality and her only comment was "What took so long; we knew years ago." My mother has been my best friend and a constant source of support and strength.

When I went through the controversy at school, I realized that when I resolved that something had to be done— that I had to respond—it was just today's version of those timeless words my parents shared with me all those years ago: "If it's meant to be, it's up to me." ∎

Diane Abbitt

Embrace who you are. Regardless of whether you think other people will like you or not, be true to yourself.

I'm Diane and I'm a lawyer.

I was raised in a very Orthodox Jewish household. My parents, first-generation Americans, had my life planned for me. I was to go to college, become a teacher, get married, have children, stay home and raise them, go back to teaching, retire, and travel with my husband.

I followed the plan up to the "get married" part. I did not want to get married, but I was young, and I went along with the program. I got married, taught for four years and had two beautiful boys. But that's when I stopped following the rules altogether.

I came out in 1973. I had met a woman. My husband and I were best of friends with her and her husband. Remember the movie *Bob & Carol & Ted & Alice*? In the movie the two couples, who were friends, switched partners. The four of us were friends, just like in the movie, and she and I fell in love. The men did not.

All my life before I came out, I knew I was different. I knew that I loved women, but it was my secret. No one said the word *lesbian*; there was nothing on TV; no books; no organizations. But by age thirty, I knew for sure I was a lesbian. And I decided this is the way it is supposed to be.

So we moved in together, each with our two children. Our children called us the *Gaydy Bunch*.

I wanted to go to law school. So we decided to go to law school together, on one set of books. We wanted to find community. It was hard to do. We heard about and went to a newly formed lesbian mothers' group at LA NOW. We became very active in LA NOW helping to start the Lesbian and Sexuality Task Force. As I became more active in defending lesbian rights, my children's father sought custody. We ended up with a shared custody arrangement. I was lucky because at the time courts would routinely force lesbian moms to give up custody of their children.

My parents were unable to accept who I was. Coming out and then having my parents tell me how I would harm my children by living this lifestyle was so very difficult. So I told my parents that they needed to seek out a therapist who could help them understand who I was and reconcile our differences. They eventually came to understand that my coming out as a lesbian was not their responsibility, and that it was who I was. In the end, we became very close. They were proud of the work I was doing.

But as bad as that challenge was, the most difficult period for me was the AIDS crisis. I watched many young men—whom I loved—get sick and die. And I couldn't do anything about it. People who are in their thirties don't belong in hospitals, but that's where I was, sleeping there with friends who were dying.

At the same time, the Gaydy Bunch was dissolving. We had graduated from law school, started our own firm and raised the children. One of our two very best friends died of AIDS and the relationship, after twenty-three years, ended. It was a horrible, horrible time. I went into therapy trying to find a way to survive all of that pain and create a new life. I faced my losses and eventually placed the painful memories in a box that I hold dear to my heart.

I kept politically active through it all and began to create a new life for myself.

I served on the Human Rights Campaign board, the Freedom to Marry board, fought Prop 8, and saw marriage equality become law.

Now I'm happy. I'm married to a wonderful woman. I have a great family of choice. My children are productive, wonderful adults. They're my friends as well as my children. We enjoy a great relationship.

If you're going to be an activist, you must love the work. At times it wasn't fun, but I've always loved the work. The fact is, if you're true to yourself and you live your life your way, you can have the most amazing, unexpected experiences. ■

You're completely normal and okay just the way you are.

Mario Diaz

I'm in the creative world. I work as an actor and event producer, which I've been doing for more than twenty-five years. I create safe spaces and places for queer connections.

Mine was a volatile upbringing—there was divorce and even a little bit of time in a foster home. I ended up ultimately living with my single father and my sister. I ran away in my teens, but I was really running toward my chosen family. I wanted to be around people who understood me and accepted me. My father did not understand me. It was very scary for him to have a son like me. He's Colombian and embraced this old-school mentality of being a player, being a gigolo. If I had been a lady-killer, he'd be proud as punch. But being a man-killer isn't quite the same thing.

I always believed, though, within my heart and in my head that who I was was good. I never believed there was something bad going on within my heart and my desires. Looking back, I am so grateful for that.

My relationship with my dad became a driving force behind what I've done with my life, which is to bring people together to dispel the shame about our sexuality that we carry with us. I try to embrace and embody a positive, shameless, unapologetic, in-your-face sexuality. And I do it with style, with a sense of humor, and tongue-in-cheek, so it's easier for people to understand that you're okay, that we're all okay.

We struggle so much with our sexuality. It manifests in our eating disorders, our body issues, or our secrets and lies. You see it in the suicide rates among the young queers, the struggles in the trans community. Homophobia is real and it's tangible, and if you're gay you feel it on some level or another. Five guys once chased me down. They totaled my car with baseball bats while I was in it.

When you're oppressed and you suppress these feelings, and you're told that there's something unnatural about you, you have to come to terms with that. And I've known some gay people who don't ever come to terms with that.

Being queer has been one of the greatest blessings of my life. Dealing honestly with who I was and how I wanted to live in the world helped me survive—and thrive. I've made it my life's mission to help people accept themselves and feel good about who they are, particularly around their sexuality.

Sex is a beautiful thing because it is something to be celebrated, not to be feared. And there's something for everyone. No matter how harshly others might judge you for expressing your natural urges and longings, remember you're completely normal and okay just the way you are. ■

Jim Colucci

My name is Jim Colucci. I work as an author and entertainment writer.

I grew up in Wayne, New Jersey, the middle son among three boys. My older brother is developmentally disabled, and because of that I always felt that I had to be twice as good. My family already had this one challenge, and so I didn't want to add another by being a bad kid.

I felt the pressure to achieve, and so I did. But that's not always the healthiest impetus. You can't live enough for two people. I felt extra pressure to be better than any one person should have to be.

My family was always a bit old-fashioned anyway, and so they encouraged a cautious, super-conservative approach to life. To be a gay kid who wants to serve his own identity in that situation presented perhaps my greatest challenge. Things seemed set up for a clash.

Coming out for me meant I

It's a rare opportunity when somebody shows you who they really are. . . .

began cautiously and slowly to just figure it out myself, without telling anybody what was going on in my head. I had gone through college and had not come out to anyone. After graduation, I first got a job in suburban Washington, and I happened to have an out-and-proud, gay male boss. And so through him I took a few baby steps into checking out that city's vibrant gay community. But then I was transferred back to an office near my parents' home, so I moved back in with them. And that meant I certainly couldn't do any experimentation when I had to report in: "Are you coming home for dinner?"

In the meanwhile, I felt like I was watching all my friends go on with their lives. They were dating, then getting married, buying homes and having kids. And I was living at home with my parents and not dating anybody and not having a life.

Not wanting to be left behind, I started reading about the gay experience—including a memoir by the man who is now my husband. And I related so much to his story, partly because he grew up in the town next to mine. I got to meet him, and we started dating. And through my relationship with him, I began to see what life could be, incorporating a happy, gay relationship,

and realized how right that felt for me. And that gave me the confidence to say, "Okay, now I can stand up and say this is who I am."

So I came out to myself when I was twenty-six, then to my closest friends, and to my family later, in my early thirties. My family's reaction? As you might expect . . . it was terrible. But by the end of their lives, both of my parents had become more accepting. On her last Christmas, Mom was very sick. Frank was generously waiting on her hand and foot, and she said, "If I'm still around next year, you're hired." Coming from her, that was acceptance.

As I began to tackle the personal side of who I really was in my midtwenties, I knew I wanted to move into more creative work as well. As a young man I had felt pressured to prepare for a very safe career, so I majored in computer science, which I really didn't like. Now, I managed to get a new job at an advertising agency, where I would be working with numbers. It wasn't the creative side of the business, but at least I was part of an agency in New York City, where there was that exciting energy.

I've always loved television, and I wanted to write for TV. But at this point, I knew if I didn't make the leap soon, it would be too late. So I started to take some classes and to write my own material, TV pilots and "spec" scripts. I loved having the creative outlet I'd been denying myself. And I eventually got an opportunity to branch into journalism and to write about television for magazines. I kept my day job, just to be safe. But this break helped me transition to do the work I wanted to do.

As I look back on my growth as a person and as a journalist, I find so much wisdom in Maya Angelou's advice: "When someone shows you who they are, believe them the first time." So many people—especially the ones you meet in the entertainment industry—put up a façade, but every once in a while it slips and you see who they really are. If you like what you see, great. But if you don't, go running because that's what is really back there. And you don't want to waste your time. ■

… When somebody gives you a window into their soul, make sure you take a look.

EMBRACED

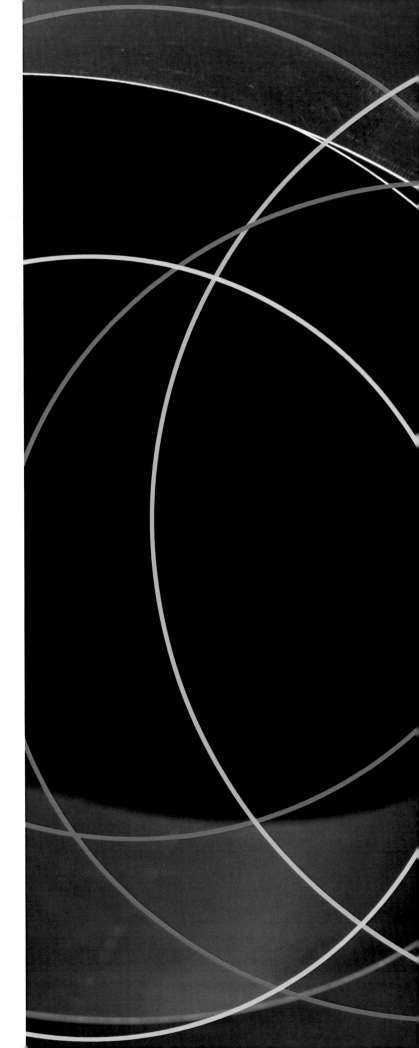

Rabbi Denise L. Eger

I'm the founding rabbi of Congregation Kol Ami in West Hollywood, California. We've grown to more than 300 households through the years, gay and straight together.

I've lived a lot of firsts. I had the honor of officiating at the first lesbian wedding in California in 2008. I've worked within Reform Judaism to open our denomination to ordaining LGBT people as rabbis. I was the first woman rabbi to be president of the Board of Rabbis of Southern California. I was the first LGBTQ person to be the president of the oldest and largest rabbinical association, the Central Conference of American Rabbis. As a rabbi now for thirty years, I've been part of a huge circle of progress. I feel very blessed.

I was born in Pennsylvania but grew up in Memphis, Tennessee.

I was very involved in our synagogue's youth movement in Memphis. We went to Jewish summer camp, and I was a song leader. My greatest challenge, however, during those years was knowing that I was lesbian. But in those years you couldn't be out and open. We had no role models. You didn't dare speak about your emotions; you stuffed them inside.

The closet is so unhealthy. Whatever your closet is, open the doors and let the fresh air in.

I enrolled at Memphis State to study music. My interest in music prompted me as a sophomore to interview for cantorial school in New York. They told me I didn't have enough experience and "Call us when you're thirty." So I just decided, well, maybe I should just be a rabbi who sings.

I learned about a joint undergraduate program between our seminary in Los Angeles and the University of Southern California. I applied and was accepted, so I loaded up my stuff and came to USC as a junior, not knowing a soul in California.

By the spring of my senior year I knew in my heart that I was not going to live as a straight woman. But now I began to wonder how can you be a rabbi and be gay? There were no role models.

In those years you could be kicked out of seminary if you were discovered to be gay or lesbian. I just thought, well, I'll just stay single throughout my life because I felt the calling to be a rabbi and to serve the Jewish people.

After more than five years of rabbinic school, ordination came around and I interviewed for a number of jobs in California. And you waited for "match day"—just like in medical school. I got called before the scheduled time. They told me, "We really liked you, Denise, but we can't hire you because you're a lesbian." I didn't come out in the process. I never said it to anybody. But I always said I lived in a plexiglass closet during those years.

So I didn't get any of those jobs specifically because I was a lesbian, not because of my skill set, or my talents, or my intelligence.

And then—miracle of miracles—I got a job as the rabbi of Beth Chayim Chadashim here in LA, which is the world's first LGBT synagogue.

I was twenty-eight years old and newly ordained. It was summer 1988, the height of the AIDS crisis. Again, I had no role models to show me how to be a gay rabbi serving a community in deep trauma and crisis. I was going to the hospital visiting, even feeding, people. These young men who were my age—in their twenties and early thirties—were wasting away, just skin and bones. I'm taking care of people with AIDS, running support groups, doing lots and lots of funerals, and trying to build a congregation at the same time.

I was trying to help people *not* compartmentalize their lives when I was just starting the process of *not* compartmentalizing my life. What I taught then and what I still teach today is that the closet is so unhealthy. Whatever your closet is, it's not healthy to keep it in your life. If you're hiding who you are, you can't lead a fulfilling in-touch, psychologically healthy life. So I was continuously trying to help people integrate who they are, in particular their sexual orientation, with their Judaism, with their humanity.

My guiding mission statement is written on my prayer shawl and in my office around a window that looks out at the sanctuary. And that is a quote from the Prophet Micah in the Bible: "What does God require of you only to do justice, to love compassion and walk humbly with your God." ■

Gloria Bigelow

My name is Gloria Bigelow. I'm a stand-up comedian. My superpower by day is working with children—I teach performing arts to kids, second through fifth grade. At night I tell jokes.

I grew up in a more than predominantly—let's say almost entirely—white suburb of Pittsburgh called Mt. Lebanon. There was my mom, my dad, and my brother. We were an upper middle-class black family surrounded by white folks.

It mattered to my mother what the white folks thought of us. We had to be on time for everything. We had to work harder than they do. We had to show up before they do. We had to do all of these things so that we could be seen as just good enough by our white peers. And, of course, that does a number on you.

My parents wanted us to have a really great and privileged life, and I feel like I have had that in many ways. But I still have a lot of conditioning to undue. Sometimes it's silly things like don't eat watermelon in front of white people. I do play my music loud in the car sometimes just because when I was growing up it was like, "Don't play your music because white people think all black people play their music loud in the car."

I'm of the age when I should just be able to do what I want to do and not have to be worried about the white gaze or the straight gaze or anybody else's gaze on me.

Find your own strength, create your own agenda, and become your own advocate, and those who can will get on board and those who can't … have got to go.

In my life I can say there were two things that were most difficult to overcome. One was the death of my father. I was twenty-two when my father had a massive heart attack at the age of fifty-four. His death blindsided my family. I was a daddy's girl and very close to him. So when he passed away I lost what felt like my primary parent because he was the person I was closest to. I thought I would always be a person who walked around full of sorrow feeling incomplete my whole life. It's not all roses now, but I feel like I have gotten to the other side of that—to a point where I can remember the joy of having had my father for twenty-

two years. I allowed myself to feel all of the feelings, even if it took years—and it did.

The second most difficult challenge was coming out. I didn't come out until I was twenty-five. I had known I was not straight from the time I was going through puberty, like twelve. And I remember writing it in my journal, and then scratching it out, because I didn't want my brother to find it and read it. And I remember driving with my mom one day and I asked her, "What would you do if I were gay?"

And she was like, "Oh, Gloria, there's so many worse things you could be. You could be an unkind person, you could snatch people's bags, you

could be mean-spirited."

So in my head I thought that she'd be okay.

I went through high school and then started college. I did all the things that I was supposed to be doing. I dated the boys and became a cheerleader. I had a boyfriend. But I knew that I wasn't straight. I was working at a gay coffee shop. I was always hanging out at a gay women's bar called My Sister's Room. It wasn't that I was in denial; I was just not ready. I just couldn't relate to the images of queer women that I saw. Would I have to wear like combat boots the rest of my life? Or fatigues?

It was my twenty-fifth birthday when I came out. I didn't

want to shut down the feelings anymore. I literally said to myself, "You might have to carve your own way and figure out how to still be who you are and a black lesbian woman." I soon found out that there's a whole bunch of us who are just like me.

The tough part was on the other side of that—dealing with my family. When I came out I was like extra loud and proud. I was super gay. It didn't occur to me that my mom would actually have a tough time with this because she told me when I was thirteen that there are so many worse things that I could turn out to be. We were driving in the car, and she's trying to set me up with some guy. I said, "I have a girlfriend." And she was like, "What?"

"I have a girlfriend. I'm dating this woman."

My mom lost her shit. She was not the "there's so many worse things" mom that I remember. She was now, "You're ruining your life, you're ruining my life. You're ruining your family's life."

I became in her eyes an investment gone wrong. Our relationship was strained for many years. My brother thought that I was hurting her by being gay. The whole family was very messed up over it. I was devastated and sad. I had already lost my father, and now I felt like I had lost my mom and my brother.

I got to the point when I remember saying to myself that I wish she would stop wanting to change me. And then I thought I should stop trying to change her too. We're gonna coexist.

Then things really shifted. After I came back from graduate school, I was living with my mom and she was doing that whole you were raised Catholic and you shouldn't be doing this thing. And then I just was like, "If you can't get it together and accept me then you're going to miss out on my life. I'm going to have a really good life. I'm going to have great parties and great children, and you're going to miss it if you can't figure out a

way to love me as I am."

Then something flipped in her, and she completely changed. Now my mom goes on gay cruises with me. She was at my birthday party with a house full of lesbians. She's just a mom. She went off on somebody who said something about someone being an ugly dyke. "You don't get to say those kinds of things," she told the person.

I was able to face up to my mother and turn her around because I felt really good about who I am and told her she needed to get on board with that.

And that's how I am now about everything. When I accepted myself fully and walked into my own greatness, things got better for me. If you can't be okay with me being who I am, then we don't need to coexist. ∎

Whether you're a superstar or the last person on the bench, everybody has a role to play, and it's about something greater than just yourself.

My name is Jason Collins. When I graduated from college in 2001, I was drafted into the NBA and played professional basketball for thirteen years. It was a lifelong dream come true. I went to the finals twice and to the playoffs ten of those thirteen years.

Today, I work for the NBA's Social Responsibility Department, otherwise known as NBA Cares. We produce a lot of events—many for the next generation on their way up. We recently rolled out the Jr. NBA, which offers instruction to help boys and girls around the world become better basketball players—and better people. After every event I've done, I walk away with a smile on my face—it's all about giving back and it feels great.

I grew up here in the Los Angeles area, in the San Fernando Valley. My parents sacrificed everything for me and my twin brother, Jarron. He and I played basketball, baseball, soccer, tennis, foot-ball—you name it. But in eighth grade we decided to focus on basketball because that was the sport we loved the most and were best at. Our immediate goal was to earn a Division I college scholarship—and our ultimate goal was to play in the NBA. So we worked hard on and off the court and ultimately we put ourselves in a position to pick and choose which school we wanted to go to. We both chose Stanford. And we both went to the NBA.

Along the way, I think there have been two major challenges I've had to face. The first was dealing with career-threatening injuries just as I began my career at Stanford. I got hurt in my freshman year and had two knee surgeries. Then as a sophomore I dislocated my wrist on my shooting hand, and I had to relearn how to shoot a basketball. As difficult as this period was, it taught me an important lesson: don't ever think that you have to face something so difficult alone. Rely on the people who truly care about you.

The matriarch of our family was my grandmother: picture an older woman with a Bible in one hand and a belt in the other. She'd tell us to overcome adversity through love, through the strength of our family and our community, and through hard work. Following her advice, I actually became a better shooter after my injury than I was before. I had to work that much harder because I wanted to achieve my goal of playing in the NBA, and I wanted to graduate from Stanford because basketball doesn't last forever.

Just as I am proud of being black and proud of being tall, I am proud of being gay. Getting to fully accept myself, though, took a long time and became my second, and very personal, challenge. I knew that I was gay since junior high school.

When I was a teenager, my uncle came out. The reaction from some family members wasn't positive. And I remember thinking to myself, "If this is what they're saying about him, what will they say about me one day?" So I never told anyone until I was thirty-three. I kept telling myself, "I'm going to find the right woman who will make these feelings go away." And of course that's not how it works.

So in late 2011 I first came out to a family member—it was my aunt with whom I always felt a special connection. I eventually told my parents and told more and more family members. Most everyone was accepting. A few would ask, "We accept you, we love you, but do you have to be public about it? Can't you just live your life in a dignified, private way?"

And I said to them, "That is not the person I was raised to be."

I remember welcoming Sally Ride, who was the first female American astronaut and a graduate of my high school, when she returned to address the student body. And it wasn't until years later, when her obituary appeared, that she came out publicly. And as I read it, I thought to myself, "That high school kid who was struggling back then would have really appreciated hearing at that assembly that she was a member of the LGBT community, and that it hadn't stopped her from achieving her dreams and accomplishing so much as a trailblazer."

And so when family members told me I could have this dignified private life, I thought, "That may be true, but that doesn't help that kid who's struggling. I don't want to come out in my obituary. That's not going to be me."

Each time I was traded to a new team it was like getting a new job and having to introduce yourself. For me the CIA cover story was, "Yes, I'm dating a girl who works and goes to school and can't come to visit." I got tired of telling a lie. I told my agent that I'm a gay man and I want to tell my story. So we decided to get it out there after the 2013 season. In the meantime I was living in, and playing for, Washington as the Supreme Court argued two huge same-sex marriage cases that would have a direct impact on my happiness in life. I remained silent and it just about killed me.

When I did tell my story, I wasn't met with rejection. The people who mean the most to me in my life were behind me and supported me. I was always taught to be a good teammate. I know what it's like to be the big dog on the team. I also know what it's like to be the last guy on the bench. The team is made stronger when we're all pulling for each other and with each other. ■

Jonah Wolf Ragir

My name is Jonah Wolf Ragir. I'm a student at UC Berkeley studying philosophy—with a long-term goal of becoming a professor.

I grew up in Los Angeles, in the same house that my mom lives in today. It was a pretty challenging upbringing. My folks got divorced by the time I was eight, and although both of my parents tried their best, no one was prepared for the problem that I was. I was born with really serious health problems and, on top of all that, I was seriously behaviorally challenged. It would be an understatement to call me emotionally disturbed and uncontrollable.

Everything changed when I first discovered alcohol. On my first night of drinking as a kid, I had an entire bottle of a Glenlivet 12 and was transformed. I thought, "This is the greatest thing that's ever happened to me, and I'll give anything to feel like this. I'm going to do this every day for the rest of my life." It gave me the comfort I needed to finally start living. Amidst all that, I came out (initially as bisexual).

When I was seventeen, I fell in love with someone who wound up changing my life. Throughout our four-year relationship, they identified as a woman, a man, and no gender. For me, that was never the issue. What *was* the issue was that their heroin addiction dominated our relationship. Despite that, everyone who knew us assumed that we were going to wind up together.

And then I was home for Thanksgiving break from school, and I got a call from my partner's mom. She told me that they found my partner dead in their apartment. They had overdosed. Amidst that, the death of my grandfather, and my own substance abuse issues, I collapsed and dropped out of college. My life shrunk to the head of a pin.

But I've always had a hunger to be better than I am. That's underwritten my whole life. At that point in my life, it was about *you* needing to love *me*, and I wasn't okay unless you did.

That hunger, despite it being for all the wrong reasons, led me out of that pit. That way out, as contrived as it sounds,

Life is better when

was spirituality. I went to an observance of a holy night of the Baha'i Faith, and I had what Christians would call a born-again moment. I was sitting in the aisle during the Declaration of the Báb, and I broke down weeping. That moment led to meeting a man who encouraged me to get sober. From there, I joined the faith, sobered up, and began the journey to live an authentic life that I'm still on today.

I'd say there are two things that have helped me to adjust and live really in a joyful context—even in the face of serious misfortune. It's that I'm totally willing, and I just so genuinely live life totally present to the moment.

I identify as queer. A very simple part of why that is is that, aside from my partner and me, the exact details of my sexuality are nobody's business. The more complicated truth is that I was empowered to have my sexuality be unimportant to me. Most of the LGBTQ+ friends I talk to feel like a huge part of their identity is rejecting the prejudice of homophobes, transphobes, etc. Embracing their sexuality meant living in spite of people, and that became an important part of their identity.

Instead, I was privileged to have a family that left space for me to explore myself. All anyone around me was concerned with was whether I was living a full, authentic life. My sexuality was just another part of me, and frankly a rather private, unimportant part. I'm deeply aware that being able to live like that is a rare privilege. Who I am is normal. To be blunt, who I/us sleep with, or want to be in a relationship with, should not be anyone's business other than who I want to do it with and be with. Straight people don't have to announce their sexuality, and neither do I. I'm just me. ■

I'm improving myself.

Dominic Montelongo

My name is Dominic Joseph Montelongo, and I help create all visual displays at Saks Fifth Avenue, Beverly Hills.

I use composition, lighting, fashion and fine art techniques to bring corporate directives to life. I love the artistic challenge as well as collaborating with others.

I grew up in San Gabriel in the '70s, and my parents divorced when I was a child. The traumatizing part for me was when my mother remarried. I was gay, and my stepfather was a Mormon head football coach who didn't want to know how to interact with a gay child.

I was tormented at school, as well as at home, causing me to have serious thoughts of suicide. The only thing that prevented that from happening was knowing it would have destroyed my beloved mother.

Growing up through those tough times of the '80s, the music and fashion coming from London, being broadcast on MTV, gave me a glimpse of what life could be like. I moved to Venice Beach, got a job at a vintage shop, studied at Santa Monica College, and then received a partial scholarship to attend Pasadena Art Center. It was here my skills as a three-dimensional artist were honed.

Do not be afraid of the darkness. Embrace it.

When you are ready to emerge, you'll be transformed.

There have been extreme highs and lows since then.

I have traveled to the UK, France, Spain, Sweden, and Argentina. I was headhunted and took a plum visual job at Barneys, then suffered a corporate layoff. After being unemployed for a year and a half, my partner and I decided to make a mutually terrible year into a very memorable one and decided to get married.

It was during this time that I realized the importance of going for a daily run in order to clear my head and think things out in order to stay mentally positive.

Life flies by, and I try my very hardest to not take one day for granted. ■

Quinn Fontaine

I'm Quinn Alexander Fontaine. I say yes to life, one day at a time. My passion is truth telling, doing what I call inspirational comedy—not quite inspirational speaking and not quite stand-up comedy—just talking to people in the moment about real stuff and whatever comes up. Pretty much like what I'm doing right now.

I was born in the Philippines. My dad was in the service; he was in three of the four military branches. We ended up moving every six months to a year. We finally landed in Virginia where I grew up and went to school, kindergarten through twelfth grade.

I knew from a pretty young age that I was a boy trapped in a girl's body. This was in the seventies and eighties. There were no 1-800 help lines; there was no one to reach out to. I couldn't talk to anybody. I would pray every night going to sleep that I would wake up in the right body. I was a girl on the outside, but I knew I was a boy inside—a straight trans guy. There was no word for me. The word *transgender* didn't come into the common vernacular until the early or mid-1990s. I couldn't find a place to plug in; I didn't know where I could find "my people." That caused me deep-rooted pain.

It's never too late to be your authentic self.

But there was more about me that would find its way to the surface.

When I was thirty-seven, I went on a trip with my dad. Cellular memory kicked in and I began to piece my life together. I realized that I had been sexually violated as a baby and through my toddler years. I experienced memory flashes and a lot of sensory memory. Every single trigger, every single sexual kink, everything made sense at that moment. So even before I knew I was in the wrong body as a baby, my introduction to the world was a feeling that it's not safe to have a body, any body, and I had carried around the most venomous amount of rage and a matching level of sadness. I always thought I felt that way because we grew up poor, or I was in the wrong body, or a whole list of other *maybes*. It never fully made sense until that early childhood trauma surfaced.

I started to see a therapist three times a week, for about three months. An image of me as a baby in diapers came up once in a therapy session. I shut it down, knowing I couldn't handle it. A lot of trauma survivors dissociate as a defense mechanism. You leave your body; you separate.

That same night I got online looking for sex. I found a woman who wanted to act out a consensual rape scene. I had never wanted that before, but I wanted to act out what had happened to me. Afterwards she said, "You want some crack?" I was like, "Okay, great." I'm thinking, "Fuck life." I told my therapist I couldn't do intense therapy and smoke crack. I told her I would call her when I'm done. Fast forward a year and three months: I called my therapist and told her, "I can't seem to die, and I don't know how to live. What's next?" She said, "Rehab."

I got online and found a center in another state that specialized in intensive trauma resolution. It took me three days to get up, put the pipe down, and get on the plane. I knew I was going to die if I didn't go, and I knew I couldn't help myself. I crawled into town as a crack-addicted, alcoholic, pill-popping sex addict. I stayed there for three months as an inpatient. I decided to start my life over, to try life on life's terms, to live life for the first time ever.

I entered the program as a woman. I knew I was trans but couldn't deal with that yet because on some level I thought I had to handle the trauma first to get to the transgender piece. They're both body-based, however, and were, in fact, intertwined. I concluded that being trans at that time on this planet was part of my trauma and, like most trauma, is healable. But you must do the work around it. You can't just sit back and hope it will take care of itself. And with a friend's gentle prodding, I started the process of transitioning.

I've been off crack cocaine for more than twelve years. It took me forever to put down the pills, pot, and alcohol. But I've finally cleaned that up. And I'm four years into my transition; I just celebrated my four-year "man-niversary." It has saved my life.

I'm an optimist. I love people. I love laughing. I love making people laugh. But more than that, I'm here to help people feel. And I'm here to remind people to tell their truth because that's where the power is. ∎

Frank Rodriguez

I'm a creative director with an advertising company. I do graphic design, writing … whatever marketing the project needs.

I grew up in the Midwest and have one brother.

I would say my family life was fairly harmonious. Our family grew up together. We expanded our horizons together, not only through the businesses my parents managed but also through travel, art, and intellectual pursuits.

But it wasn't always easy.

My greatest challenge was growing up gay and keeping my secret. No one knew. My friends didn't know, my parents didn't know, none of my relatives knew. My brother, who is five years older than I, came out when I was a senior in high school. And so the pressure was on me to be the straight one, get married, and have kids.

So you're constantly presenting someone who's not really who you are. If you're black and someone calls you a name at school, you go home and you vent with your family, and all agree, "That person's a jerk." But if you get called a name because someone suspects your gay, you can't tell anyone. You suffer silently. You have no support from your family or community. You're entirely alone.

Feeling forced to hide out in your own family has tormented many gays from my generation. And people don't realize how toxic it can be.

I didn't come out until I was twenty-seven. My parents had already processed much of this with my brother. They realized this doesn't have to do with how they brought up their kids. This is bigger than that. I think too that they knew other parents who had lost kids to suicide and drugs. I think they were grateful that they enjoyed a good relationship with me and my brother and that we were employed and not on drugs.

So it's all relative.

But one thing kept me going. My brother had instilled in me that people who were truly individuals were the coolest people. I loved rock music and underground culture. My heroes were all the people who were the antiheroes. As young as thirteen, I knew I didn't want to be the country club guy. I wanted to go to New York and photograph rock stars and write for *Rolling Stone*.

But the culture that I was always interested in didn't reflect my sexuality. When

I moved to Los Angeles, I couldn't find my tribe because I didn't find gay people who liked what I liked. The gay people I met looked like West Hollywood. I thought of their value system and aesthetics as completely alien.

It took me a few years to meet key people who introduced me to more people. And that's when I opened a nightclub with a couple of very creative friends. The club put the punk world together with the gay world. It was an unusual space where gay people came for live music and to be themselves, and straight people came to be exposed to all this madness. So that was a really big thing in my life.

All of a sudden the people who I knew were out there came, and I had a community for the first time. I felt like I belonged.

In all the work I've done, my idea has been that the envelope for what LGBTQ is should be bigger. The culture was very much owned by New York and by people who couldn't pass. And so they designed the culture to represent them. People who didn't fit in were ostracized.

People would tell me, "Oh, you know, you like cars because that's your beard."

And I was like, "My beard is on my face. I've liked cars since I was three years old. I'm not doing this to try to appear straight. And I like punk rock music because I like the music. I'm not doing it to appear straight."

So for me, my job has been to expand the culture: to show how you can be a woodworker from Oklahoma and still be gay. Everyone should have a voice and everyone should be represented. ∎

If you don't find the community you belong to, you have to create it.

Estevan Jose Montemayor

I'm Estevan Montemayor. I'm deputy chief of staff to Los Angeles City Council member David Ryu. I'm also the president of the board of the Christopher Street West Association.

My job is to work with our board to realize our vision as an organization. Our most well-known event is the LA Pride Festival and Parade in West Hollywood. Last year we wanted to draw attention to the Supreme Court's recent decision involving a cake maker's refusal to work with a gay couple and how that decision opens the door for discrimination. And so Cake and Art, a small business in West Hollywood, donated a five-tier cake—white on the outside, rainbow inside. Our grand marshal, Michaela Mendelsohn, who's a trans woman and activist, cut the cake with her wife. And the big takeaway was that we can have our cake and our equal rights too.

I was raised by a single mom who emigrated from Mexico when she was still in grade school. My father was a migrant worker. He picked fruit and vegetables all his life with his brothers, sisters, and my grandmother.

My mom didn't speak a word of English when she came here. She later returned to school and became a leader in her community, teaching women about self-empowerment. And my grandmother went to community college and then a four-year college, probably in her fifties. She became a teacher and then ran for city council in her small town in Oregon. In my mother and my grandmother, I saw very strong role models who came from nothing but decided they would make something of their lives.

My upbringing was difficult, as much as it was full of love. My mom did everything and anything to support me and my older brother. She was mom and dad. My father was an alcoholic, and my mother was a victim of domestic violence. I saw and heard things that really have taken a long time for me to try to move past. My brother had his own struggles. He dealt with substance abuse and issues with the law. I was raised around all of that, and it really made me think about who I was supposed to be and how I should be that person. It was difficult.

Once I did come out as a gay Latino boy, there was only acceptance and love from my family. In my own mind, though, I created self-doubt and judgments about myself. I was assuming things that I never should have assumed. I was playing too much the victim. I saw the different caricatures of gay men in TV and film. I knew about the AIDS crisis, and I knew that those were gay men dying. I wondered is that what happens to gay men? I struggled internally with anxiety. Would other people accept me, whether from the gay community or not? I was trying to prove that I was worthy of what I wanted to accomplish. My biggest struggle was to overcome judgments that I had put in my own way, which were unnecessary and unfounded.

I looked at my mother and my grandmother who had come from nothing and yet achieved so much. I told myself that you would do them a disservice and other people like yourself if you do not take on the mantle, move forward, and do your best to be your best.

Just keep going. Life gets tough. Everything is tough. You need tough people to deal with tough situations. If you sit there and stew in it, it's just shitty. If you keep going, you'll get through it and life gets better. ■

When you stumble, keep faith. And when you're knocked down, get right back up and never listen to anyone who says you can't or shouldn't go on.

(from Hillary Clinton)

ACKNOWLEDGMENTS

I have many people to thank for their help in making *LGBTQ OF STEEL*.

My husband, whose idea it was to represent my artistic theme in the pages of this book featuring a different community from the first book.

Thank you to all the subjects of the book who spent their valuable time coming to the studio for a shoot and baring their souls in an interview, and dealing so creatively with a meaningful piece of steel.

To my son Marc/Senor Amor who populated this book through his vast friend network and a lot of hard work and many hours. Also thank you for assisting in every shoot and being sure all went smoothly.

Thanks to those who gave design advice, assistance and editing support.

A deep thanks to family and dear friends who always have words of encouragement.

INDEX